SO YOU WANT
TO SING JAZZ

SO YOU WANT TO SING

A GUIDE FOR PROFESSIONALS

A PROJECT OF THE NATIONAL ASSOCIATION OF TEACHERS OF SINGING

So You Want to Sing: A Guide for Professionals is a series of works devoted to providing a complete survey of what it means to sing within a particular genre. Each contribution functions as a touchstone work for not only professional singers, but students and teachers of singing. Titles in the series offer a common set of topics so readers can navigate easily the various genres addressed in each volume. This series is produced under the direction of the National Association of Teachers of Singing, the leading professional organization devoted to the science and art of singing.

So You Want to Sing Music Theater: A Guide for Professionals, by Karen S. Hall, 2013.

So You Want to Sing Rock 'n' Roll: A Guide for Professionals, by Matthew Edwards, 2014.

So You Want to Sing Jazz: A Guide for Professionals, by Jan Shapiro, 2015.

SO YOU WANT TO SING JAZZ

A Guide for Professionals

Jan Shapiro

Allen Henderson
Executive Editor, NATS

A Project of the National Association of
Teachers of Singing

ROWMAN & LITTLEFIELD
Lanham • Boulder • New York • London

Published by Rowman & Littlefield
A wholly owned subsidiary of The Rowman & Littlefield Publishing Group, Inc.
4501 Forbes Boulevard, Suite 200, Lanham, Maryland 20706
www.rowman.com

Unit A, Whitacre Mews, 26-34 Stannary Street, London SE11 4AB

British Library Cataloguing in Publication Information Available

Library of Congress Cataloging-in-Publication Data

Shapiro, Jan, author.
  So you want to sing jazz : a guide for professionals / by Jan Shapiro.
     pages cm. – (So you want to sing)
  Includes bibliographical references and index.
  ISBN 978-1-4422-2935-8 (pbk. : alk. paper) – ISBN 978-1-4422-2936-5
(ebook) 1. Singing–Instruction and study. 2. Jazz vocals–Instruction and
study. I. Title.
  MT868.S43 2016
  782.42165'143–dc23

                                                        2015028351

∞™ The paper used in this publication meets the minimum requirements
of American National Standard for Information Sciences—Permanence of
Paper for Printed Library Materials, ANSI/NISO Z39.48-1992.

Printed in the United States of America

*To my very first musical influence, my mom, Virginia Shapiro,
and to my dad, Earl Shapiro, who encouraged me
by slipping cash into my pocket for voice lessons.*

And to Mrs. Lucille Edmonds, my first voice teacher.

CONTENTS

LIST OF FIGURES

FOREWORD

So You Want to Sing Jazz: A Guide for Professionals, the third book of the "So You Want to Sing" series, is an important addition to the series collection. I first met Jan Shapiro in 2000 when she chaired the voice department at the Berklee College of Music and hired me to teach in the voice department. At that time, she was already a leader in the field of jazz, both as a teacher and singer. Her long experience as a jazz singer and teacher means she has the depth of knowledge and experience necessary to write the jazz book. Singers (both beginning and experienced), teachers, and coaches will find valuable information on jazz history, pedagogy, style, and much more from a woman who knows her stuff.

Ever since meeting Jan back in 2000, I have greatly admired her intellectual prowess, her courage, and her honesty. She "tells it like it is," and I have always appreciated that part of her personality. When Jan agreed to write the jazz book, she had written a few journal articles but never a book or a dissertation. I knew she didn't fully realize the challenges that lay ahead, but when that reality set in, she persevered and worked with passion, drive, and dedication on this important project. Her knowledge is thorough and timely. There are few, if any, jazz pedagogy books that encompass the scope of her book, one of its unique characteristics. Even though she struggled at times, she was always willing to work with me to figure out what needed to be accomplished. She never lost her sense of humor and was gracious when I had to push her. She always remained positive and optimistic, the consummate professional.

I believe that by attempting to teach singing with this important series, we will make many important discoveries about how to teach all kinds of singing in new ways. Putting forth our best efforts in these books is the only way to find out. I am extremely proud to have Jan included in the project and am thrilled at her accomplishment!

—Karen S. Hall

ACKNOWLEDGMENTS

I wish to thank former series editor Karen Hall for giving me the opportunity to write this book and her constant encouragement, patience, and eagle eye. To Sophie Innerfield, my writing coach, whose editing and dedication to this project made this book possible. Thank you, Sophie!

Thank you to my friends and family for their support, to all the jazz musicians I have worked with and known, to all of my jazz singer colleagues, and to the jazz singers of the future.

INTRODUCTION

As a young musician, I did not discover jazz right away—or at least not what I understand jazz to be now. Both of my parents loved the music from the 1940s, so I grew up listening to the vocalists who sang in the Big Band era. Ella Fitzgerald was among these singers, but as a teenager I didn't pay much attention to whether or not a singer would scat. Typically I just liked to sing songs along with the artist without thinking too much about what made their technique or style stand out. My musical tastes varied from Broadway musicals to folk, pop, and soul. I did not think of the 1940s singers as jazz. But then again growing up in Festus, Missouri, I did not really know what that meant.

I knew I wanted to be a singer even as a very small child. As I grew up, I heard everything from Big Band music of the 1940s to Mahalia Jackson to musical theater playing on the home stereo. I also heard my mom sing along with the music or play piano and sing. By two years old, I started humming along. I read music by the age of six. At fifteen I began formal voice lessons.

In the 1960s and early 1970s, Barbra Streisand, Shirley Bassey, and Julie Andrews were the singers to whom I could relate the most because I was a lyric soprano with a natural vibrato. In my teens I went through a folk phase and taught myself guitar. If I sang lower, I could kind of sound more like a folk and pop singer. Of course, this was in my own inexperienced vocalist view.

When I studied music in college, I started to play and sing with the guitar in a few clubs. While in school, I had the opportunity to work with a band as the lead singer. I was still a little self-conscious about singing pop up-tempos. But when it came to singing ballads, I really milked them. I did not really think about style so much in my early days; I just sang. I worked hard on developing my voice with good classical training, but I could not figure out how to apply this to pop or jazz styles. As I had been taught, I sang the exact melody with the exact rhythm, exactly as written.

Eventually I left my musical studies in college to tour with a band. I sang six nights a week, four hours per night, performing around the country. When I traveled and worked with the band, we would often record ourselves to listen back and see how we could improve our performances. I remember wanting to sing a song Ella Fitzgerald made famous—her version of Cole Porter's "Just One of Those Things." I listened and listened to Ella. One night I decided I would try to emulate the style of Ella singing. It was one of the nights that we recorded our performance. A few days after, I listened to the recording of me singing. I thought I did everything just like Ella, but to my surprise and horror it did not sound like I thought it would. When I listened to the recording, I felt that I sounded like Julie Andrews trying to scat instead of Ella Fitzgerald! To truly understand jazz, I learned, was an ongoing progression and learning experience, experimenting with different registers of my voice, vocal delivery, and phrasing. I also learned so much from the great musicians I worked with and the experienced jazz singers who mentored me along the way.

This book was written for those who want to know more about jazz singing. It includes information about the history and development of jazz, vocal science and vocal health, the characteristics of jazz singing versus other kinds of singing, developing our jazz ears and how to listen to jazz, the Great American Songbook, rhythmic and melodic improvisation, scat, elements of a successful jazz vocal performance, and jazz singing as a career. I hope this book helps you find your voice as I found mine, and that you enjoy the journey!

ONLINE SUPPLEMENT NOTE

So You Want to Sing Jazz features an online supplement courtesy of the National Association of Teachers of Singing. Visit the link below to discover additional exercises and examples, as well as links to recordings of the songs referenced in the book.

http://www.nats.org/So_You_Want_To_Sing_Jazz.html

A musical note symbol ♪ in this book will mark every instance of corresponding online supplement material. Follow the link above and click on the corresponding chapter to access links, recordings, and exercises.

1

THE HISTORY OF JAZZ AND ELEMENTS OF JAZZ SINGING

SLAVERY AND THE CULTURAL ORIGINS OF THE BLUES

To learn how to sing jazz, first you need to know how to sing the blues. When we think of blues, we think of sadness. Blues songs are about misery and hardship and are deeply melancholic and emotional. The best blues singers bring deep emotion into their performances so the audience can feel and experience the song's meaning in a real, visceral way. Before attempting to sing the blues, it's a good idea to sharpen your ears by listening to early blues singers like Ma Rainey, Bessie Smith, Ethel Waters, Blind Lemon Jefferson, and Charles Patton, among many others. What is it about singing the blues that differs from singing other styles?

The origins of the blues go all the way back to the seventeenth century. During the two hundred years between the 1600s and the mid-1800s, slave traders from North America pillaged West Africa's various kingdoms, tribes, and kinship groups. Displaced slaves were brought by slave traders to port cities near the Mississippi River as they awaited further transportation or sale. They had been torn from their homeland, separated from their loved ones, and endured human rights abuses beyond all imagining. This deep historical trauma—and the finding of community within this painful context—is at the root of the blues.

One of the most prominent slave-trading ports in the south was New Orleans. During the 1700s, the majority of slaves that were brought to New Orleans were from West Africa, which includes modern-day Senegal, Guinea, Gambia, Sierra Leone, Liberia, Ivory Coast, Ghana, Togo, Benin, Nigeria, Cameroon, Gabon, Congo, and Zaire (Southern 1997, 3). Slave traders who traveled to West Africa were struck by the importance of music and dance across different West African groups. Much of the knowledge we have about West African music and dance from this time period comes from slave trader chronicles and letters (Southern 1997, 4). For example, in West African tribes, men were the primary instrumentalists. One of the main instruments used by these tribes were drums of varying sizes. These drums would be played simultaneously. However, each drum had a different pitch and each drum, large and small, was played at the same tempo but in different rhythmic patterns, called polyrhythms. Women joined in by singing and dancing, and others would join in by clapping and stomping their feet. For some of the major life events such as birth, death, and marriage, women would play instruments as well as sing. There was a song and dance for all major events in West African life. Music was a cornerstone of culture and communication across the region.

Starting in the eighteenth century, slaves in New Orleans were typically allowed one day off from work on Sundays. They would gather in Congo Square, singing songs and clapping and playing rhythms from their native West Africa. Even though the New Orleans slaves were not necessarily from the same groups in West Africa, they shared the musical traditions from across the region. Using improvised drums made of "gum stumps" and sheepskin heads, they would play polyrhythms, creating a backdrop for singers and dancers to join in (Southern 1997, 137). Southern describes the scene:

> The dancing would build up in excitement, becoming wilder and more frenzied as the afternoon wore on, until men and woman would fall fainting to the ground. Their places were quickly taken, however, by other couples. . . . The vocal music accompanying the dances obviously comprised chants rather than genuine songs, and these were repeated over and over again for as long as five or six hours. As much as fatigue, it was the incessant chanting and the exciting music that sent the dancers into a state of ecstasy and eventually caused them to "fall fainting to the ground." (Southern 1997, 137–38)

During these chants, a singer would sing or chant a line, and the rest of the group would sing it back in a call and response pattern. The musical phrases varied in length, and the musical scale the slaves sang was different than a traditional Western scale and was unique to the West African region. This scale, which is the origin of the modern blues scale, had a different note pattern and sound. Based on note patterns within this scale, the singer would hold out one note and slide into the next. These gatherings created an opportunity for different West African musical traditions to meld together into something unique to New Orleans.

Other musical and cultural influences came together in Congo Square as well. After the Haitian Revolution in 1804, a number of slaves and free Black people came to New Orleans from Haiti. Many of these people practiced voodoo, a religious tradition particular to the region of West Africa that is now Benin. Voodoo ceremonies almost always included dance. These voodoo dances, tied to different religious celebrations throughout the year, became a part of the Congo Square gatherings. This added another musical and dance element to the evolving musical culture of slaves in New Orleans.

In addition to the gatherings in Congo Square, slaves drew upon their native musical traditions as they picked cotton in the fields. During this repetitive, backbreaking work, they would often sing out to each other. One person might decide to shout and sing out a hello to someone in a field away, and others would join, following certain patterns. This was a way of communicating with one another and became known as a field holler. Sung a cappella, a blues shout, a work song, and a field holler are similar. The holler or work song would be partially sung with varying pitches and varying levels of dynamics. A holler could also incorporate a loud cry or moan. One person would shout or sing loudly enough to be heard, and someone else would reply back in the same manner. The difference in hollers was the lyrical content, the subject matter, and even location. There are few recordings of these early hollers. However, there are some recordings available from *Southern Mosaic: The John and Ruby Lomax 1939 Southern States Recording Trip*.

Continuing to incorporate West African scale patterns and rhythms, slaves would also sing and chant the end of the workday. They would gather with homemade instruments made up of string or wire scraps for strings or shaped metal to form a simplistic kind of horn. A wooden barrel with a stretched cloth or animal hide across the top often served as the drum. A yard party gathering or a parade would attract people to come together and share their songs. Music was a deeply meaningful form of communication, recreation, and artistic expression for slaves, as well as the many immigrants that came to America via New Orleans, including Spanish, American Indian, and Creole. This mix of cultures became a major influence on American blues and jazz as we know it today. However, the music and culture of African slaves had the deepest impact on jazz. This book provides only the briefest introduction to this complex history. For an in-depth exploration, please read Eileen Southern's *The Music of Black Americans: A History*.

Characteristics of the Blues-Singing Elements of Vocal Improvisation: Rhythm, Pitch, and Dynamics

From these origins, the blues as we know them today developed through the second half of the nineteenth century as the Civil War, and slavery, ended. The traditional blues song is composed of what is known as a blues chord progression, shown in figure 1.1.

Blues singing involves singing a melody that coincides with this chord progression. Although traditional blues singers used part or all of a blues

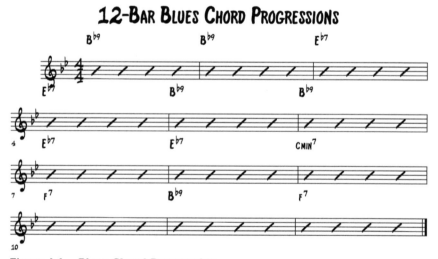

Figure 1.1. Blues Chord Progression

scale pattern when singing the blues, it is worth noting that our analysis of the chord progressions and scales they were using came later on, as musicologists and scholars began to analyze this uniquely American musical genre. Early blues artists were not writing or performing for a scholarly audience. Blues singers improvised by hearing the standard twelve-bar progression, unconsciously using what we call the blues scale as a guide. This scale and the improvisational characteristics of blues singing—including shouting, storytelling, and expressive conversational delivery—grew holistically out of the musical traditions of African American slaves (figure 1.2).

In the early twentieth century, African American blues singers started performing to a wider audience, performing in theaters, bars, and traveling tent shows. Blues singers were accompanied mostly by piano and guitar, with a clarinet or horn player added in as time went on. Blues singing has always been different from traditional classical or music theater performance. Listening to blues singers and instrumentalists captures our attention because of the true-to-life and sometimes comical lyrics. But if we listen with jazz ears, we will start to hear more than just the words. The blues singer has a unique way of emphasizing the words and notes in each song and adds dynamics in a way that is very specific to the genre. He or she can add emotional flourishes such as growls, moans, or cries or even speak a word aloud. The best blues singers make the audience feel the music deep in their bones.

Singers Ma Rainey and Bessie Smith were two of the earliest well-known traveling blues singers in the South and Midwest, touring during

Figure 1.2. Blues Scale

the 1920s and 1930s. When we listen to the early recordings of Bessie Smith with piano, the rhythm played by the pianist is unlike a classical Western European approach. In blues piano, we hear the pianist using the left hand to keep the time in mostly stride style, hitting the bass keys of the piano. The pianist then plays a chord in the left hand that coincides with the melody played with the right hand. To gain a better idea of how the pianists played early blues, listen to Roosevelt Sykes and early recordings of Jelly Roll Morton, Fats Waller, and James P. Johnson. All listening examples can be found at the National Association of Teachers of Singing (NATS) website, www.nats.org. Recorded examples of early blues piano styles include: Bessie Smith singing "Keeps on a-Rainin'," Jelly Roll Morton playing "The Pearls," and Fats Waller accompanying blues singer Alberta Hunter in "You Can't Do What My Last Man Did." ♪

Blues bands added more instruments as the style developed. A band could be composed of piano, banjo, tuba, string bass, and drums. A guitarist or banjo player would strum every beat within a four-beat measure. A cornet, trumpet, trombone, or clarinet could also be added to the band. The added horn player or players would improvise the melody in such a way that it would interact with the vocalist singing the melody. At the same time the bass and drums maintained the tempo. This allowed the pianist the freedom to accompany a vocalist or an instrumental solo without having to consistently keep the rhythmic beat in the left hand. This led to more interpretive and improvisational piano playing as the style developed.

However, when there was only a pianist accompanying the singer, the pianist's left hand beat was steady and strong while the right hand played a countermelody or an embellishment complementary to the sung melody. A blues singer would often lay back behind the beat instead of singing on the downbeat with each phrase. This skill is part of vocal rhythmic improvisation. To begin to understand this way of singing, listen to a blues or jazz song that you already know. For example, listen to early blues singer Bessie Smith sing "St. Louis Blues" or "Downhearted Blues." After listening a few times, start at the beginning of the recording and tap your foot to the beat you hear. Even if the singer or horn player you hear comes in at the same time you are tapping your foot, called the downbeat, wait after you hear the chord and then sing the first word within the song. This is what it means to be laying back behind the phrase, a characteristic of blues and jazz singing. ♪

In addition to the rhythmic aspects of vocal improvisation, blues singers also improvise with pitch and dynamics. Part of the improvisation is the singing of blue notes—notes lowered slightly from the expected pitch within a scale—within a phrase for emphasis or expression. Lyrics as well as notes are improvised to get across the singer's story. For example, blues singers will often slide into or off of notes, purposely leaning into a word or bending the pitch on a note for emphasis. Some of the notes and words within the phrase are almost spoken on pitch until the end of the phrase, which adds texture and color to the lyrics and melody. Classic vocal blues sometimes entails a kind of moaning to express sadness or pain or a shouting style for emphasis and emotion. The singer will sometimes speak a phrase or a word—for example, "let me tell you about it"—and then go back to singing. While the band plays one rhythm, the blues singer will vary their phrases in a conversational way. The singer does not plan out how they will use these elements ahead of time; they improvise using a combination of these dynamic elements. In time, singers develop their own voice and intuition, using these elements in their own unique way.

In many cases, a traditional blues singer utilized all the above elements depending on the music and lyrics. The format of blues chord progression and the style of singing the blues influenced all vocal music from jazz to rock. Some classical blues singers were able to cross over as early jazz singers while other blues vocalists preferred staying with traditional blues. To general audiences, singing blues may mean that one has to have a strong and forceful gritty sound with a low timbre voice. In actuality, just as many early blues singers had lighter, clear voices such as Ethel Waters, Clara Smith, and Blind Lemon Jefferson, as well as the huskier sound of singers like Bessie Smith. More important than the timbre or tone of the voice is the blues delivery and expression—utilizing emphasis on specific words and subtle use of accents, stressing a particular word or leaning on it, and laying back behind the beat. The following and all future recorded examples can be found at the NATS website, www.nats.org. Examples of early blues performances are:

- "Heebie Jeebies," Louis Armstrong
- "Downhearted Blues," Bessie Smith

- "My Handy Man," Ethel Waters
- "C and a Blues," Peetie Wheatstraw
- "Walkin Blues," Robert Johnson
- "You're Gonna Miss Me When I'm Gone," Muddy Waters ♪

Recorded examples of the blues shout style of singing are:

- "Hide And Seek," Big Joe Turner
- "Love Me Baby," Jimmie Witherspoon
- "Alimony Blues," Eddie Cleanhead Vinson
- "Let the Good Times Roll," Louis Jordan
- "Shout Sister Shout" and "River Stay Away from My Door," sung by the Boswell Sisters (soloist Connie Boswell) ♪

Other listening examples that showcase a combination of the above elements are:

- "Honey Where You Been So Long," Ma Rainey
- "Come On Home," Alberta Hunter
- "Weary Woman's Blues," Memphis Minnie
- "Graveyard Bound Blues," Ida Cox
- "I Can't Be Satisfied," Big Bill Bronzy
- "Honey You Don't Know My Mind," Barbecue Bob ♪

Additional Elements of Blues Singing

Articulation and Verbalizing

Blues singers have a specific way of utilizing their lips, teeth, and tongue to articulate and verbalize lyrics. Try speaking the preceding sentence as you normally would. Then try using your lips more than usual on the same phrase. You'll notice that your sound comes out a bit more forcefully and the words are clearer. Blues singers use this technique of melodic articulation and spoken words within a song to affect how the audience hears and listens to specific words within the lyrics. A singer might decide to overarticulate or exaggerate a specific word to be more emphatic and bring attention to the meaning of the particular word. We likely do the same thing with words if we are angry or upset! Overarticulation of a song's lyrics goes along with blues singers' conversational delivery. It makes what the singer is saying to us real and meaningful and helps carry the singer's voice further—and its emotions deeper.

Rhythmic Phrasing

Classical musicians play music as it is written, playing or singing the melody with the exactly notated notes and rhythms. In contrast, the majority of early blues instrumentalists and singers did not read music. Blues musicians would embellish the melody and would change the melody and the rhythms within a phrase as a form of expression. The same song will often sound different in different performances and recordings.

The following recorded examples of rhythmic phrasing include:

- "Crazy Blues," Mamie Smith
- "Get Up in the Mornin'," Leadbelly
- "Murder's Gonna Be My Crime," Sippie Wallace
- "Dinah" (with a scat solo), Louis Armstrong
- "I'm Gonna Move to the Outskirts of Town," Jimmy Rushing ♪

Vibrato vs. Straight Tone Conversational Singing

Some blues singers sing with a full voice and vibrato. Other blues singers sing in a conversational or talking delivery so that the vibrato is slight, at the end of a phrase, at the peak of a phrase, or absent—no vibrato at all. When singers use a full voice and vibrato, we can hear a rounder or fuller sound with vibrato at the end of each phrase. Conversational and talking delivery is more laid back. However, the idea of "laid back" is truly one of degree in blues. In both of the recorded examples below, the phrasing is relaxed and laid back and it sounds as if the singers are talking to us. The textures of their voices are very different, but both songs and singers are unambiguously blues. A recorded example of singing with vibrato is Bessie Smith in "Gulf Coast Blues," and a recorded example of straight tone conversational phrasing is Blind Lemon Jefferson in "Baker Shop Blues." ♪

THE SWING ERA

The blues was not the only African American–created musical genre that evolved during the nineteenth century. There were several distinct musical strains developing during this time, and their interactions are complex. For the purposes of this book, we focus on the blues. However, in order to transition to early swing, we must take a brief look at ragtime and African American brass bands as well.

Ragtime

After the Civil War and freedom, many African Americans were able to purchase instruments for their families. Music maintained its importance for freed slaves, and as African Americans built lives for themselves in America post-slavery, they also built new musical traditions. Keyboard instruments—organs in particular, because they were cheaper than pianos—were especially popular (Southern 1997, 314). This predilection for keyboard instruments created a fairly large population of piano players, and pianos or organs were a common part of African American social lives from the late nineteenth century onward. Pianos were often used as the sole musical accompaniment in many bars or dance halls in African American neighborhoods. Ragtime, which is an umbrella term for several strains of dance hall piano in the late nineteenth and early twentieth centuries, is written in 2/4 or 4/4 meter, with a syncopated melody (a melody whose accents fall in between the prominent one and three beats played in the bass) that causes the listener to anticipate the rhythm and follow the beat. Ragtime composers drew their influences not only from antebellum (pre–Civil War) music and West African polyrhythms, but also from more traditional composers such as John Philip Sousa, whose marches were well known during that time. The result was a lively, fun style that became wildly popular. The syncopated melody and steady beat fueled dance halls and set the foundations for another new genre of dance music to flourish. A recorded example of ragtime is Scott Joplin performing the "Maple Leaf Rag." ♪

African American Brass Bands

By the end of the nineteenth century, community brass bands were widespread in the United States. New Orleans had an especially strong brass band tradition, and most of the area's brass bands were made up of African American players. Brass bands played a number of different kinds of music, suitable to any occasion: popular music for dancing, such as waltzes and polkas; hymns for solemn occasions such as funerals; and marches for parades and civic events. They were extremely versatile. At some point in the early twentieth century, players in these traditional bands started to experiment with blues elements, using their cornets and clarinets to mimic the dirty tones and bent blue notes of traditional blues singers. Once this fusion of older styles from very different traditions began in New Orleans, it was unstoppable. Early syncopated dance music spread across the nation, and many of the big names in early swing came out of the tradition of brass bands. Recorded examples of New Orleans brass bands include "Dr. Jazz," "High Society," and "Panama." ♪

The Beginning of Swing

In the 1920s and 1930s, American blues vocalists and their bands remained very popular. However, a new form of music emerged (a constant theme in the early twentieth century!), which included and built upon elements of blues, ragtime, and brass bands. This new form of music was called swing. Swing bands had different instruments than blues bands. More bands used an acoustic string bass, a piano, and drums while adding additional instruments such as guitar, trumpet, and clarinet. The swing feel (also called the groove) literally made one feel a sort of swaying motion and was easy to dance to—you'll notice this theme come up constantly in the early days of jazz! Dance halls were a major form of entertainment, and people were hungry for new dancing music.

Swing band members would interact with one another to establish a groove. As the band played, the big band vocalist would sing. The blues delivery and characteristics were still in the vocals, but the instrumentation, song lyrics, and underlying rhythm were different. The swing feel set up a steady rhythm for the vocalist and horn players, which allowed them to improvise rhythmically as well as melodically, as in a traditional blues band, but the new rhythmic feel led to new improvisational styles. This new music was everywhere. In between radio skits, comedian acts, and dramas, radio stations featured live swing bands and vocalists, which helped the new style gain ground fast. Recorded examples of early swing include "King Porter Stomp" and "Sweet Rhythm."

Louis Armstrong and the Birth of Jazz

One of the most important figures in swing and early jazz was Louis Armstrong. Born into a poor family in New Orleans in 1901, Armstrong picked up odd jobs throughout his childhood, including singing on street corners. He eventually managed to teach himself how to play the cornet and received some formal education at the Colored Waif's Home for Boys in New Orleans and quickly became an expert. He was a musical prodigy whose talents were noticed by major brass band leaders in the city, and he played with several important bands in New Orleans before eventually moving north and landing in New York City in 1924.

When Louis Armstrong left New Orleans and headed north, he became known as the hot trumpet soloist in swing bands. Armstrong was also a talented vocalist who combined both his playing and his singing into his performances. He was a profoundly charismatic performer, and his influence on early jazz and swing is unmistakable. Many singers during this time period, such as Connie Boswell and Billie Holiday, borrowed the rhythmic phrasing of Louis in his horn playing and singing. The difference between blues singing and early swing was subtle. First, the band accompaniment changed the overall feel or groove of the song. Sometimes there was a two-beat groove: a feeling of two beats to a measure in a song written in 4/4 tempo. The bass player would play on beat one and three, while the guitar player or pianist might play all four beats in a measure.

Recorded examples of the two-beat groove include Louis Armstrong playing "I Ain't Got Nobody" and the Count Basie Orchestra playing "I'll Always Be in Love with You." ♪

Focus on guitarist Freddie Green, Ella Fitzgerald with Count Basie and his orchestra playing "Honeysuckle Rose," and Tony Bennett and K. D. Lang performing "Exactly Like You." ♪

The other popular groove was a straight eighth rhythm groove, which shows eighth notes written in a straight ahead pattern but played with a swing feel, meaning that the notes are not played equally. Instead, the first note is played longer than the second—but only barely. This slight extension of the first note makes a big impact. Recorded examples of a straight eighth note rhythm groove are Carmen McRae singing "Yardbird Suite" and Abbey Lincoln singing "Can You Dig It." ♪

Figure I.3.   Band and Vocalist Swing Notation

Swing vocalists had to internalize the swing rhythm but had the freedom to be interpretive with the melodic line. Vocalists of early swing incorporated blue notes, but the improvisation was more about rhythmic phrasing and subtle use of embellishments than playing with pitch. Early swing singers might start singing immediately after the first downbeat or after the first chord was played. Both the band and the vocalist would swing.

The eighth note feel in a measure of 4/4 on the written page would look like this:

EIGHTH NOTES   Shapiro

Figure I.4.   Eighth-Note Feel in 4/4

The Big Band Era

As swing music became more popular, there were more and more swing bands that showcased vocalists. In the late 1930s and throughout the 1940s, big bands—with a full horn section and singers—were the most popular musical groups in America. Big band recordings became huge hits, and by the late 1940s, the vocalists became the feature rather than the band. Singers like Frank Sinatra, Helen Forrest, and Ella Fitzgerald would no longer wait for their bands to play one or two choruses. Instead, there was a brief musical introduction by the band and the vocalist would begin to sing. The band played on the second chorus or soloed, and the vocalist came back in to sing the last chorus of the song. Their personalities and celebrity status boosted the genre.

Scat Singing

When we listen to the swing singers, we can feel the swing in the way the singer phrases the lyrics. Characteristics of the swing singers include rhythmic phrasing; conversational delivery; vibrato, little vibrato, or vibrato at the ends of each phrase; and holding a note or word over the bar line—all of which are common elements to blues, as well, but sound very different in a swing context. Singers during this era also began to improvise by emulating a horn soloist and singing hornlike riffs in a nonverbal singing style known as scat.

It is impossible to tell when scat singing began (as with many details in the origins of jazz, its birth is hard to pinpoint), but by the late 1920s, Bing Crosby and the group Rhythm Boys were improvising songs by mimicking instrument sounds from brass all the way to percussion, and Crosby soloed in a scat style. As his career progressed, he moved on to more popular music, but he does provide an early example of instrumental vocal improvisation.

In the early recordings of Ella Fitzgerald, her scat singing sounds very much like a trumpet or sax solo. In order to scat, a singer has to know the melody and chord progressions of a song very securely. The scat solo has to match the chord progressions, just as an instrumental solo would. Some big band vocalists like Ella Fitzgerald and Anita O'Day experimented with scat improvisation while other vocalists improvised using rhythmic phrasing. A recorded example of improvisational rhythmic phrasing is Anita O'Day singing "Let's Fall in Love." ♪

For the inexperienced jazz singer, scat singing can be overwhelming since it is an acquired skill. Singers from the big band era including Ella Fitzgerald and Sarah Vaughan sang constantly, often multiple shows per day. Every night the singer would sit alongside the band and hear the horn soloists. When the band played the same songs night after night, a trumpet player's solo—while improvised—might resemble the solo he or she played the night before. Singers who were with big bands would listen to the horn solos night after night and in time were able to mimic the horn player and use that as a starting point to develop original improvised solos. This worked both ways. A horn player might play off the singer's improvised solo as well!

Recorded examples of early scat singing include Bing Crosby singing "Some of These Days" and Ella Fitzgerald singing "How High the Moon." ♪

THE BEBOP ERA AND BEYOND

Starting in the 1950s, jazz bands were mostly composed of trios, quartets, quintets, and sextets. The era of the big band was over, and bands became much more pared down. Piano, bass, and drums made up the basic trio, with the option of adding other instrumentalists such as guitar, trumpet, or saxophone. During this time period, jazz shifted away from the swinging dance music of the 1940s and became music for audiences to sit and listen to. Instrumental solos took on a new prominence. A song was usually composed of one or two verses, a bridge, and then another verse, which functioned as a vehicle for solo improvisation with the possibility of additional solo choruses. Tempos could range from a ballad style, with the drummer playing brushes, to fast swing, with forceful percussion. This new style of jazz presented a challenge to vocalists, since the focus was no longer on song structure and lyrics but more on technical and improvisational mastery.

By the 1960s, more and more jazz vocalists experimented along with the jazz musicians. Instrumentalists would both play and sing. Instrumentalists Chet Baker and Clark Terry could play a horn solo with finesse as well as vocalizing in a scat style or singing lyrics. Vocalists developed more complex improvisational phrases, and the scat style became more hornlike, not always following the melody, even at the beginning of a well-known song. Jazz vocalist Betty Carter became recognized for her hornlike phrasing and interpretation. Some of the greats, whose careers spanned multiple eras of jazz—Ella Fitzgerald, Anita O'Day, and Mel Tormé, among many others—became known for their scat solos set to varied swing tempos. Singer Sarah Vaughan could also scat well, but she would also improvise with the words, bending the notes and words like an instrument or rhythmically altering a word or note. She also used tonal colors in her vocal delivery. Recorded examples of bebop era singers (note the difference from when you heard some of these singers earlier!) include:

- "One Note Samba," Ella Fitzgerald
- "Is You Is or Is You Ain't My Baby," Anita O'Day
- "Lullaby of Birdland," Mel Tormé
- "Lullaby of Birdland," Sarah Vaughan ♪

COOL JAZZ

From the mid-1950s and 1960s, another kind of jazz, called cool jazz, developed. Vocalists who took to the cool jazz style sang with a laid-back rhythm. The style was a more subdued approach than big band or bebop for both instrumentalists and singers. The vocal tone could be understated with varied, subtle use of vibrato. Often, vocalists sang with a light sound rather than a full vocal sound. Recorded examples of cool jazz include:

- "Born to Be Blue," Helen Merrill
- "Something Cool," June Christy
- "Don't Forget to Smile," Mose Allison
- "It Could Happen to You," Chet Baker ("The Prince of Cool") ♪

From a vocal perspective, there are elements of jazz singing that thread throughout all eras of jazz: bending pitch, rhythmic interpretation, and using dynamics to emphasize different words. However, when we look at all of these elements together, the defining characteristic of jazz vocalization, from the earliest blues to modern-day jazz, is improvisation. Improvisation means altering the original melody rhythm and/or note values written by the composer or lyricist, varying the emphasis on one note or word, and changing the overall tone and delivery within a song.

Improvisation doesn't necessarily come naturally. It comes from a place of technical mastery and confidence that allows a singer to play with a song in a way that enhances the performance. The greatest jazz singers sang the same songs thousands of different ways before landing on the versions we hear today in recordings—and even those represent only one interpretation from one performance. The possibilities are endless. Jazz singers have infinite improvisational options in regard to their own interpretation, whether it is laid-back phrasing on a ballad, subtle embellishment added to the written melody, soloing on the second chorus with lyrics to scat singing, or using all of these options at different times. Learning how to sing jazz means learning how to improvise in your own unique way.

BIBLIOGRAPHY

Southern, Eileen. (1997). *The Music of Black Americans: A History*. 3rd edition. New York: W. W. Norton.

2

SINGING JAZZ AND VOICE SCIENCE

Scott McCoy

This chapter presents a concise overview of how the voice functions as a biomechanical, acoustic instrument. We will be dealing with elements of anatomy, physiology, acoustics, and resonance. But don't panic: the things you need to know are easily accessible, even if it has been many years since you last set foot in a science or math class!

All musical instruments, including the human voice, have at least four things in common, consisting of a *power source, sound source* (vibrator), *resonator*, and a system for *articulation*. In most cases, the person who plays the instrument provides power by pressing a key, plucking a string, or blowing into a horn. This power is used to set the sound source in motion, which creates vibrations in the air that we perceive as sound. Musical vibrators come in many forms, including strings, reeds, and human lips. The sound produced by the vibrator, however, needs a lot of help before it becomes beautiful music—we might think of it as raw material, like a lump of clay that a potter turns into a vase. Musical instruments use resonance to enhance and strengthen the sound of the vibrator, transforming it into sounds we identify as a piano, trumpet, or guitar. Finally, instruments must have a means of articulation to create the nuanced sounds of music. Let's see how these four elements are used to create the sounds of singing.

PULMONARY SYSTEM: THE POWER SOURCE OF YOUR VOICE

The human voice has a lot in common with a trumpet: both use flaps of tissue as a sound source, both use hollow tubes as resonators, and both rely on the respiratory (pulmonary) system for power. If you stop to think about it, you quickly realize why breathing is so important for singing. First and foremost, it keeps us alive through the exchange of blood gases—oxygen in, carbon dioxide out. But it also serves as the storage depot for the air we use to produce sound. Most singers rarely encounter situations in which these two functions are in conflict, but if you are required to sustain an extremely long phrase, you could find yourself in need of fresh oxygen before your lungs are totally empty.

Misconceptions about breathing for singing are rampant. Fortunately, most are easily dispelled. We must start with a brief foray into the world of physics in the guise of *Boyle's Law*. Some of you no doubt remember this principle: the pressure of a gas within a container changes inversely with changes of volume. If the quantity of a gas is constant and its container is made smaller, pressure rises. But if we make the container get bigger, pressure goes down. Boyle's law explains everything that happens when we breathe, especially when we combine it with another physical law: *nature abhors a vacuum*. If one location has reduced pressure, air flows from an area of higher pressure to equalize the two, and vice versa. So if we can create a zone of reduced air pressure by expanding our lungs, air automatically flows in to restore balance. When air pressure in the lungs is increased, it has no choice but to flow outward.

As we all know, the air we breathe goes in and out of our lungs. Each lung contains millions and millions of tiny air sacs called *alveoli*, where gases are exchanged. The alveoli also function like ultra-miniature versions of the bladder for a bag pipe, storing the air that will be used to set the vocal folds into vibration. To get the air in and out of them, all we need to do is make the lungs larger for inhalation and smaller for exhalation. Always remember this relationship between cause and effect during breathing: we inhale because we make ourselves large; we exhale because we make ourselves smaller. Unfortunately, the lungs are organs, not muscles, and have no ability on their own to accomplish this feat. For this reason, your bodies came from the factory with special muscles designed to enlarge and compress your entire thorax (ribcage), while simultaneously moving your lungs. We can classify these muscles in two main categories: any muscle that has the ability to increase the volume capacity of the thorax serves an *inspiratory* function; any muscle that has the ability to decrease the volume capacity of the thorax serves an *expiratory* function.

Your largest muscle of inspiration is called the *diaphragm* (figure 2.1). This dome-shaped muscle originates from the bottom of your sternum (breastbone) and completely fills the area from that point around your ribs to your spine. It's the second-largest muscle in your body, but you probably have no conscious awareness of it or ability to directly control

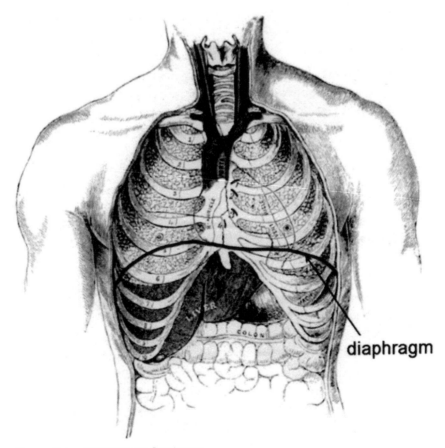

diaphragm

Figure 2.1. Diaphragm Anatomy

it. When we take a deep breath, the diaphragm contracts and the central portion flattens out and drops downward a couple inches into your abdomen, pressing against all of your internal organs. If you release tension from your abdominal muscles as you inhale, you will feel a gentle bulge in your upper or lower belly, or perhaps in your back, resulting from the displacement of your innards by the diaphragm. This is a good thing and can be used to let you know you have taken a good inhalation.

The diaphragm is important, but we must remember that it cannot function in isolation. After you inhale, it relaxes and gently returns to its resting position through an action called *elastic recoil*. This movement, however, is entirely passive and makes no significant contribution to generating the pressure required to sustain phonation. Therefore, it makes no sense at all to try to "sing from your diaphragm"—unless you intend to sing while you inhale, not exhale!

Eleven pairs of muscles assist the diaphragm in its inhalatory efforts, which are called the *external intercostal* muscles (figure 2.2). These muscles start from ribs one through eleven and connect at a slight angle downward to ribs two through twelve. When they contract, the entire thorax moves up and out, somewhat like moving a bucket handle. With the diaphragm and intercostals working together, you are able to increase the capacity of your lungs by about three to six liters, depending on your gender and overall physical stature; thus, we have quite a lot of air available to power our voices.

Eleven additional pairs of muscles are located directly under the external intercostals, which, not surprisingly, are called the *internal intercostals* (figure 2.2). These muscles start from ribs two through twelve and connect upward to ribs one through eleven. When they contract, they induce the opposite action of their external partners: the thorax is made smaller, inducing exhalation. Four additional pairs of expiratory muscles are located in the abdomen, beginning with the *rectus* (figure 2.2). The two rectus abdominis muscles run from your pubic bone to your sternum and are divided into four separate portions, called *bellies* of the muscle (lots of muscles have multiple bellies; it is coincidental that the bellies of the rectus are found in the location we colloquially refer to as our belly). Definition of these bellies results in the so-called ripped abdomen or six-pack of body builders and others who are especially fit.

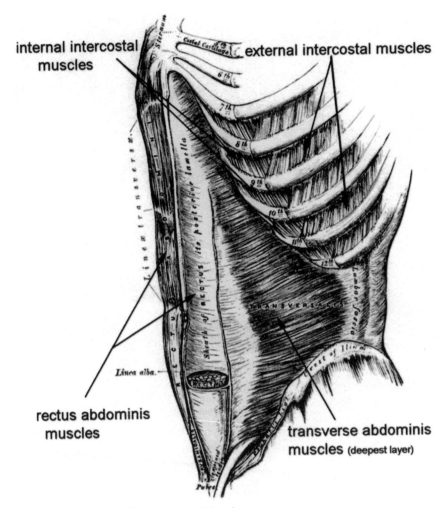

internal intercostal muscles

external intercostal muscles

rectus abdominis muscles

transverse abdominis muscles (deepest layer)

Figure 2.2. External Intercostal Muscles

The largest muscles of the abdomen are called the *external obliques* (figure 2.3), which run at a downward angle from the sides of the rectus, covering the lower portion of the thorax, and extend all the way to the spine. The *internal obliques* lie immediately below, oriented at an angle that crisscrosses the external muscles. They are slightly smaller, beginning at the bottom of the thorax, rather than extending over it. The deepest muscle layer is the *transverse abdominis* (figure 2.3), which is oriented with fibers that run horizontally. These four muscle

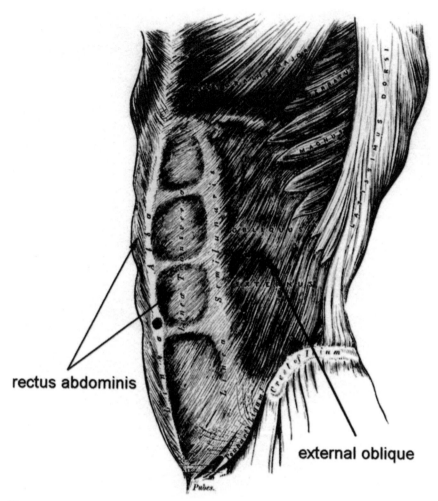

rectus abdominis

external oblique

Figure 2.3. **Muscles of the Abdomen**

pairs completely encase the abdominal region, holding your organs and digestive system in place while simultaneously helping you breathe.

Your expiratory muscles are quite large and can produce a great deal of pulmonary or air pressure. In fact, they easily can overpower the larynx. Healthy adults generally can generate more than twice the pressure that is required to produce even the loudest sounds; therefore, singers must develop a system for moderating and controlling airflow and breath pressure. This practice goes by many names, including breath support, breath control, and breath management, all of which rely on the principle of *muscular antagonism*. Muscles are said to have an antagonistic relationship when they work in opposing directions, usually pulling on a common point of attachment, for the sake of increasing stability or motor control. You can see a clear example of muscular antagonism in the relationship between your biceps (flexors) and triceps (extensors) when you hold out your arm. In breathing for singing, we activate inspiratory muscles (e.g., diaphragm and external intercostals) during exhalation to help control respiratory pressure and the rate at which air is expelled from the lungs.

One of the things you will notice when watching a variety of singers is that they tend to breathe in many different ways. You might think that voice teachers and scientists, who have been teaching and studying singing for hundreds, if not thousands of years, would have come to agreement on the best possible breathing technique. But for many reasons, this is not the case. For one, different musical and vocal styles place varying demands on breathing. For another, humans have a huge variety of body types, sizes, and morphologies. A breathing strategy that is successful for a tall, slender woman might be completely ineffective in a short, robust man. Our bodies actually contain a large number of muscles beyond those we've already discussed that are capable of assisting with respiration. For an example, consider your *latissimi dorsi* muscles. These large muscles of the arm enable us to do pull-ups (or pull-downs, depending on which exercise you perform) at the fitness center. But because they wrap around a large portion of the thorax, they also exert an expiratory force. We have at least two dozen such muscles that have secondary respiratory functions, some for exhalation and some for inhalation. When we consider all these possibilities, it is no surprise at all that there are many ways to breathe that can produce beautiful singing. Just remember to practice some muscular antagonism—maintaining a degree of inhalation posture during exhalation—and you should do well.

LARYNX: THE VIBRATOR OF YOUR VOICE

The larynx, sometimes known as the voice box or Adam's apple, is a complex physiologic structure made of cartilage, muscle, and tissue. Biologically, it serves as a sphincter valve, closing off the airway to prevent foreign objects from entering the lungs. When firmly closed, it also is used to increase abdominal pressure to assist with lifting heavy objects, childbirth, and defecation. But if we gently close this valve while we exhale, tissue in the larynx begins to vibrate and produce the sounds that become speech and singing.

The human larynx is a remarkably small instrument, typically ranging from the size of a pecan to a walnut for women and men, respectively. Sound is produced at a location called the *glottis*, which is formed by two flaps of tissue called the *vocal folds* (aka vocal cords). In women, the glottis is about the size of a dime; in men, it can approach the diameter of a quarter. The two folds are always attached together at their front point but open in the shape of the letter V during normal breathing, an action called *abduction*. To phonate, we must close the V while we exhale, an action called *adduction* (just like the machines you use at the fitness center to exercise your thigh and chest muscles).

Phonation only is possible because of the unique multilayer structure of the vocal folds (figure 2.4). The core of each fold is formed by muscle, which is surrounded by a layer of gelatinous material called the *lamina*

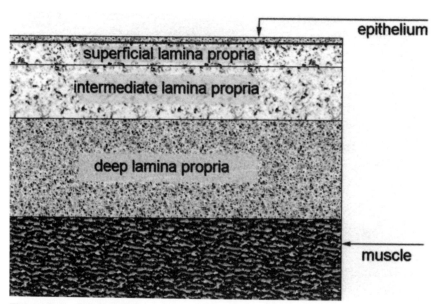

Figure 2.4. Vocal Folds

propria. The *vocal ligament* also runs through the lamina propria, which helps to prevent injury by limiting how far the folds can be stretched for high pitches. A thin, hairless epithelial layer that is constantly kept moist with mucus secreted by the throat, larynx, and trachea surrounds all of this. During phonation, the outer layer of the fold glides independently over the inner layer in a wavelike motion, without which phonation is impossible.

We can use a simple demonstration to better understand the independence of the inner and outer portions of the folds. Explore the palm of your hand with your other index finger. Note that the skin is attached quite firmly to the flesh beneath it. If you poke at your palm, that flesh acts as padding, protecting the underlying bone. Now explore the back of your hand. You will observe that the skin is attached quite loosely—you easily can move it around with your finger. And if you poke at the back of your hand, it is likely to hurt; there is very little padding between the skin and your bones. Your vocal folds combine the best attributes of both sides of your hand. They provide sufficient padding to help reduce impact stress, while permitting the outer layer to slip like the skin on the back of your hand, enabling phonation to occur. When you are sick with laryngitis and lose your voice (a condition called *aphonia*), inflammation in the vocal folds couples the layers of the folds tightly together. The outer layer no longer can move independently over the inner, and phonation becomes difficult or impossible.

The vocal folds are located within the five cartilaginous structures of the larynx (figure 2.5). The largest is called the *thyroid cartilage*, which is shaped like a small shield. The thyroid connects to the *cricoid* cartilage below it, which is shaped like a signet ring—broad in the back and narrow in the front. Two cartilages that are shaped like squashed pyramids sit atop the cricoid, called the *arytenoids*. Each vocal fold runs from the thyroid cartilage in front to one of the arytenoids at the back. Finally, the *epiglottis* is located at the top of the larynx, flipping backward each time we swallow to prevent food and liquid from entering our lungs. Muscles connect between the various cartilages to open and close the glottis and to lengthen and shorten the vocal folds for ascending and descending pitch, respectively. Because they sometimes are used to identify vocal function, it is a good idea to know the names of the muscles that control the length of the folds. We've already mentioned that

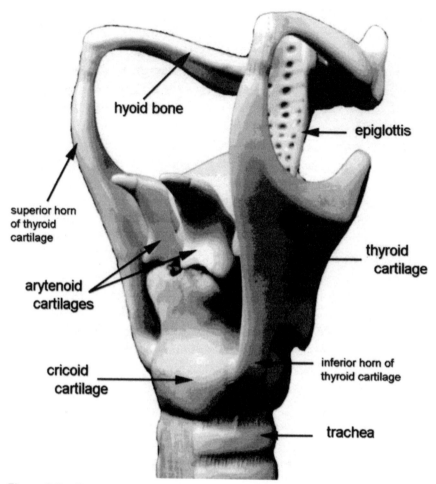

Figure 2.5. Structure of the Larynx

a muscle forms the core of each fold. Because it runs between the thyroid cartilage and an arytenoid, it is named the *thyroarytenoid* muscle (formerly known as the *vocalis* muscle). When the thyroarytenoid, or TA muscle, contracts, the fold is shortened and pitch goes down. The folds are elongated through the action of the *cricothyroid*, or CT muscles, which run from the thyroid to cricoid cartilage.

Vocal color (timbre) is created by the combined effects of the sound produced by the vocal folds and the resonance provided by the vocal tract. While these elements can never be completely separated, it is useful to consider the two primary modes of vocal fold vibration and their resulting sound qualities. The main differences are related to the relative thickness of the folds and their cross-sectional shape (figure 2.6). The first option depends on short, thick folds that come together with nearly square-shaped edges. Vibration in this configuration is given a variety of names, including *Mode 1, Thyroarytenoid* (TA) *dominant, chest mode,* or *modal voice.* The alternate configuration uses longer, thinner folds that only make contact at their upper margins. Common names include *Mode 2, Cricothyroid* (CT) *dominant, falsetto mode,* or *loft voice.* Singers vary the vibrational mode of the folds according to the quality of sound they wish to produce.

Before we move on to a discussion of resonance, we must consider the quality of the sound that is produced by the larynx. At the level of the glottis, we create a sound not unlike the annoying buzz of a duck call. That buzz, however, contains all the raw material we need to create speech and singing. Vocal or glottal sound is considered to be *complex,* meaning it consists of many simultaneously sounding frequencies (pitches). The lowest frequency within any tone is called the *fundamental,* which corresponds to its named pitch in the musical scale. Orchestras tune to a pitch called A-440, which means it has a frequency of 440 vibrations per second, or 440 *Hertz* (abbreviated Hz). Additional frequencies are included above the fundamental, which are called *overtones.* Overtones in the glottal sound are quieter than the fundamental. In voices, the overtones usually are whole number multiples of the fundamental, creating a pattern called the *harmonic series* (e.g., 100Hz, 200Hz, 300Hz, 400Hz, 500Hz, etc. or G2, G3, C4, G4, B4—note that

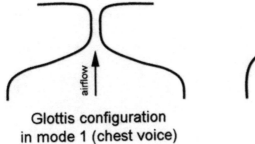

Glottis configuration
in mode 1 (chest voice)

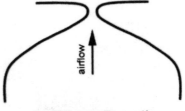

Glottis configuration
in mode 2 (falsetto)

Figure 2.6. Vocal Folds Cross-Section

pitches are named by the international system in which the lowest C of the piano keyboard is C1; middle-C therefore becomes C4, the fourth C of the keyboard) (figure 2.7).

Singers who choose to make coarse or rough sounds as might be appropriate for rock or blues often add overtones that are *inharmonic*, or not part of the standard numerical sequence. Inharmonic overtones also are common in singers with damaged or pathological voices.

Under most circumstances, we are completely unaware of the presence of overtones—they simply contribute to the overall timbre of a voice. In some vocal styles, however, harmonics become a dominant feature. This is especially true in *throat singing* or *overtone singing*, as is found in places like Tuva. Throat singers tune their vocal tracts so precisely that single harmonics are highlighted within the harmonic spectrum as a separate, whistlelike tone. These singers sustain a low-pitched drone and then create a melody by moving from tone to tone within the natural harmonic series. You can learn to do this too. Sustain a comfortable pitch in your range and slowly morph between the vowels /ee/ and /oo/. If you listen carefully, you will hear individual harmonics pop out of your sound.

The mode of vocal fold vibration has a strong impact on the overtones that are produced. In mode 1, high-frequency harmonics are relatively strong; in mode 2, they are much weaker. As a result, mode 1 tends to yield a much brighter, brassier sound.

VOCAL TRACT: YOUR SOURCE OF RESONANCE

Resonance typically is defined as the amplification and enhancement (or enrichment) of musical sound through *supplemental vibration*. What does

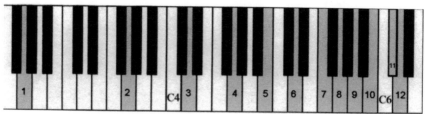

Figure 2.7. The Harmonic Series

this really mean? In layman's terms, we could say that resonance makes instruments louder and more beautiful by reinforcing the original vibrations of the sound source. This enhancement occurs in two primary ways, which are known as forced and free resonance (there is nothing pejorative in these terms: free resonance is not superior to forced resonance). Any object that is physically connected to a vibrator can serve as a forced resonator. For a piano, the resonator is the soundboard (on the underside of a grand or on the back of an upright); the vibrations of the strings are transmitted directly to the soundboard through a structure known as the bridge, which also is found on violins and guitars. Forced resonance also plays a role in voice production. Place your hand on your chest and say *ah* at a low pitch. You almost certainly felt the vibrations of forced resonance. In singing, this might best be considered your *private* resonance; you can feel it and it might impact your self-perception of sound, but nobody else can hear it. To understand why this is true, imagine what a violin would sound like if it were encased in a thick layer of foam rubber. The vibrations of the string would be damped out, muting the instrument. Your skin, muscles, and other tissues do the same thing to the vibrations of your vocal folds.

By contrast, free resonance occurs when sound travels through a hollow space, such as the inside of a trumpet, an organ pipe, or your vocal tract, which consists of the pharynx (throat), oral cavity (mouth), and nasal cavity. As sound travels through these regions, a complex pattern of echoes is created; every time sound encounters a change in the shape of the vocal tract, some of its energy is reflected backward, much like an echo in a canyon. If these echoes arrive back at the glottis at the precise moment a new pulse of sound is created, the two elements synchronize, resulting in a significant increase in intensity. All of this happens very quickly—remember that sound is traveling through your vocal tract at more than seven hundred miles per hour.

Whenever this synchronization of the vocal tract and sound source occurs, we say that the system is *in resonance*. The phenomenon occurs at specific frequencies (pitches), which can be varied by changing the position of the tongue, lips, jaw, palate, and larynx. These resonant frequencies, or areas in which strong amplification occurs, are called *formants*. Formants provide the specific amplification that changes the raw, buzzing sound produced by your vocal folds into speech and singing. The vocal tract is capable of producing many formants, which are labeled sequentially by ascending pitch. The first two, F1 and F2, are used to create vowels; higher formants contribute to the overall timbre and individual characteristics of a voice. In some singers, especially those who train to sing in opera, formants three through five are clustered together to form a super formant, eponymously called the *singer's formant*, which creates a ringing sound and enables a voice to be heard in a large theater without electronic amplification.

Formants are vitally important in singing, but they can be a bit intimidating to understand. An analogy that works really well for me is to think of formants like the wind. You cannot see the wind, but you know it is present when you see leaves rustling in a tree or feel a breeze on your face. Formants work in the same manner. They are completely invisible and directly inaudible. But just as we see the rustling leaf, we can hear, and perhaps even feel, the action of formants through how they change our sound. Try a little experiment. Sing an ascending scale beginning at B-flat3, sustaining the vowel /ee/. As you approach the D-natural or E-flat of the scale, you likely will feel (and hear) that your sound becomes a bit stronger and easier to produce. This occurs because the scale tone and formant are on the same pitch, providing additional amplification. If you change to an /oo/ vowel, you will feel the same thing at about the same place in the scale. If you sing to an /oh/ or /eh/ and continue up the scale, you'll feel a bloom in the sound somewhere around C5 (an octave above middle-c). /ah/ is likely to come into its best focus at about G5.

To remember the approximate pitches of the first formants for the main vowels, ee-eh-ah-oh-oo, just think of a C-Major triad in first inversion, open position, starting at E4: ee = E4, eh = C5, ah = G5, oh = C5, and oo = E4 (figure 2.8). If your music theory isn't strong, you could use

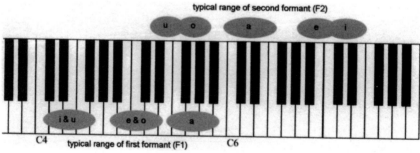

Figure 2.8. C-Major Triad, First Inversion

the mnemonic "every child gets candy eagerly." These pitches might vary by as much as a minor third higher and lower but no farther: once a formant changes by more than that interval, the vowel that is produced *must* change.

Formants have absolutely no preference for what they amplify—they are indiscriminate lovers, just as happy to bond with the first harmonic as the fifth. When men or women sing low pitches, there almost always will be at least one harmonic that comes close enough to a formant to produce a clear vowel sound. The same is not true for women with high voices, especially sopranos, who routinely must sing pitches that have a fundamental frequency *higher* than the first formant of many vowels. Imagine what happens if she must sing the phrase "and I'll leave you forever," with the word "leave" set on a very high, climactic note. The audience won't be able to tell if she is singing *leave* or *love* forever; the two will sound identical. This happens because the formant that is required to identify the vowel /ee/ is too far below the pitch being sung. Even if she tries to sing *leave*, the sound that comes out of her mouth will be heard as some variation of /ah/.

Fortunately, this kind of mismatch between formants and musical pitches rarely causes problems for anyone but opera singers, choir sopranos, and perhaps ingénues in classic music theater shows. Almost everyone else generally sings low enough in their respective voice ranges to produce easily identifiable vowels.

Second formants also can be important, but more so for opera singers than everyone else. They are much higher in pitch, tracking the pattern oo = E5, oh = G5, ah = D6, eh = B6, ee = D7 (you can use the mnemonic "every good dad buys diapers" to remember these pitches) (figure 2.8). Because they can extend so high, into the top octave of the piano keyboard for /ee/, they interact primarily with higher tones in the natural harmonic series. Unless you are striving to produce the loudest unamplified sound possible, you probably never need to worry about the second formant; it will steadfastly do its job of helping to produce vowel sounds without any conscious thought or manipulation on your part.

If you are interested in discovering more about resonance and how it impacts your voice, you might want to install a spectrum analyzer on your computer. Free (or inexpensive) programs are readily available for download over the Internet that will work with either a PC or Mac computer. You don't need any specialized hardware—if you can use Skype or FaceTime, you already have everything you need. Once you've installed something, simply start playing with it. Experiment with your voice to see exactly how the analysis signal changes when you change the way your voice sounds. You'll be able to see how harmonics change in intensity as they interact with your formants. If you sing with vibrato, you'll see how consistently you produce your variations in pitch and amplitude. You'll even be able to see if your tone is excessively nasal for the kind of singing you want to do. Other programs are available that will help you improve your intonation (how well you sing in tune) or enhance your basic musicianship skills. Technology truly has advanced sufficiently to help us sing more beautifully.

MOUTH, LIPS, AND TONGUE: YOUR ARTICULATORS

The articulatory life of a singer is not easy, especially when compared to the demands placed on other musicians. Like a pianist or brass player, we must be able to produce the entire spectrum of musical articulation, including dynamic levels from hushed pianissimos to thunderous fortes, short notes, long notes, accents, crescendos, diminuendos, and so on. We produce most of these articulations the same way instrumentalists do, which is by varying our power supply. But singers have another layer of articulation that makes everything much more complicated; we must produce these musical gestures while simultaneously singing words.

As we learned in our brief examination of formants, altering the resonance characteristics of the vocal tract creates the vowel sounds of language. We do this by changing the position of our tongue, jaw, lips, and sometimes palate. Slowly say the vowel pattern ee-eh-ah-oh-oo. Can you feel how your tongue moves in your mouth? For /ee/, it is high in the front and low in the back, but it takes the opposite position for /oo/. Now slowly say the word *Tuesday*, noting all the places your tongue comes into contact with your teeth and palate and how it changes shape as you produce the vowels and diphthongs. There is a lot going on in there—no wonder it takes so long for babies to learn to speak!

Our articulatory anatomy is extraordinarily complex, in large part because our bodies use the same passageway for food, water, air, and sound. As a result, our tongue, larynx, throat, jaw, and palate are all interconnected with common physical and neurologic points of attachment. Our anatomical *Union Station* in this regard is a small structure called the *hyoid bone*. The hyoid is one of only three bones in your entire body that do not connect to other bones via a joint (the other two are your *patellae*, or kneecaps). This little bone is suspended below your jaw, freely floating up and down every time you swallow. It is a busy place, serving as the upper suspension point for the larynx, the connection for the root of the tongue, and the primary location of the muscles that open your mouth by dropping your jaw.

Good singing—in any genre—requires a high degree of independence in all these articulatory structures. Unfortunately, nature conspires against us to make this difficult to accomplish. From the time we were born, our bodies have relied on a reflex reaction to elevate the palate and raise the larynx each time we swallow. This action becomes habitual: palate goes up, larynx also lifts. But depending on the style of music we are singing, we might need to keep the larynx down while the palate goes up (opera and classical), or palate down with the larynx up (country and bluegrass). As we all know, habits can be very hard to change, which is one of the reasons that it can take a lot of study and practice to become an excellent singer. Understanding your body's natural reflexive habits can make some of this work a bit easier.

There is one more significant pitfall to the close proximity of all these articulators: tension in one area is easily passed along to another. If your jaw muscles are too tight while you sing, that hyperactivity will likely be transferred to the larynx and tongue—remember, they all are interconnected through the hyoid bone. It can be tricky to determine the primary offender in this kind of chain reaction of tension. A tight tongue could just as easily be making your jaw stiff, or an elevated, rigid larynx could make both tongue and jaw suffer.

Neurology complicates matters even further. You have sixteen muscles in your tongue, fourteen in your larynx, twenty-two in your throat and palate, and another sixteen that control your jaw. Many of these are very small and lie directly adjacent to each other, and you often are required to contract one quite strongly while its next-door neighbor

❸

VOCAL HEALTH AND
THE VOCAL JAZZ ARTIST

Wendy DeLeo LeBorgne

GENERAL PHYSICAL WELL-BEING

All singers, regardless of genre, should consider themselves as "vocal athletes." The physical, emotional, and performance demands necessary for optimal output require that the artist consider training and maintaining their instrument as an athlete trains for an event. With increased vocal and performance demands, it is unlikely that a vocal athlete will have an entire performing career completely injury free. This may not be the fault of the singer as many injuries occur due to circumstances beyond the singer's control such as singing through an illness or being on a new medication seemingly unrelated to the voice.

Vocal injury has often been considered taboo to talk about in the performing world as it has been considered to be the result of faulty technique or poor vocal habits. In actuality, the majority of vocal injuries presenting in the elite performing population tend to be overuse and/or acute injury. From a clinical perspective over the past seventeen years, younger, less experienced singers with fewer years of training (who tend to be quite talented) generally are the ones who present with issues related to technique or phonotrauma (nodules, edema, contact ulcers), while more mature singers with professional performing careers tend to present with acute injuries (hemorrhage) or overuse and misuse injuries (muscle tension dysphonia, edema, GERD) or injuries following an illness. There are no current studies documenting use and training in correlation to laryngeal pathologies. However, there are studies which document that somewhere between 35 percent and 100 percent of professional vocal athletes have abnormal vocal fold findings on stroboscopic evaluation (Korovin & LeBorgne 2009; Phyland, Oates, & Greenwood 1999; Hoffman-Ruddy, Lehman, Crandell, Ingram, & Sapienza 2001; LeBorgne, Donahue, Brehm, & Weinrich 2012; Evans, Evans, Carvajal, & Perry 1996; Koufman, Radomski, Joharji, Russell, & Pillsbury 1996; Heman-Ackah, Dean, & Sataloff 2002; Lundy, Casiano, Sullivan, Roy, Xue, & Evans 1999; Tepe, Deutsch, Sampson, Lawless, Reilly, & Sataloff 2002). Many times these "abnormalities" are in singers who have no vocal complaints or symptoms of vocal problems. From a performance perspective, uniqueness in vocal quality often gets hired and perhaps a slight aberration in the way a given larynx functions may become quite marketable. Regardless of what the vocal folds may look like, the most integral part of performance is that the singer must maintain agility, flexibility, stamina, power, and inherent beauty (genre appropriate) for their current level of performance taking into account physical, vocal, and emotional demands.

Unlike sports medicine and the exercise physiology literature where much is known about the types and nature of given sports injuries, there is no common parallel for the vocal athlete model (Yang, Tibbetts, Covassin, Cheng, Nayar, & Heiden 2012). However, because the vocal athlete utilizes the body systems of alignment, respiration, phonation, and resonance with some similarities to physical athletes, a parallel protocol for vocal wellness may be implemented/considered for vocal athletes to maximize injury prevention knowledge for both the singer and teacher. This chapter aims to provide information on vocal wellness and injury prevention for the vocal athlete.

CONSIDERATIONS FOR WHOLE BODY WELLNESS

Nutrition

You have no doubt heard the saying "you are what you eat." Eating is a social and psychological event. For many people, food associations and eating have an emotional basis resulting in either overeating or being malnourished. Eating disorders in performers and body image issues may have major implications and consequences for the performer on both ends of the spectrum (obesity and anorexia). Singers should be encouraged to reprogram the brain and body to consider food as fuel. You want to use high-octane gas in your engine, as pouring water in your car's gas tank won't get you very far. Eating a poor diet or a diet that lacks appropriate nutritional value will have negative physical and vocal effects on the singer. Effects of poor dietary choices for the vocal athlete may result in physical and vocal effects ranging from fatigue to life-threatening disease over the course of a lifetime. Encouraging and engaging in healthy eating habits from a young age will potentially prevent long-term negative effects from poor nutritional choices. It is beyond the scope of this chapter to provide a complete overview of all the dietary guidelines for pediatrics, adolescents, adults, and the mature adult; however, a listing of additional references to help guide your food and beverage choices for making good nutritional choices can be found online at:

Dietary Guidelines for Americans: www.health.gov/dietaryguidelines/.

Nutrition.gov Guidelines for Tweens and Teens: www.nutrition.gov/life-stages/adolescents/tweens-and-teens.

Fruits and Veggies Matter: www.fruitsandveggiesmorematters.org/myplate-and-what-is-a-serving-of-fruits-and-vegetables.

Hydration

"Sing wet, pee pale." This phrase was echoed in the studio of Dr. Van Lawrence regarding how his students would know if they were well enough hydrated. Generally, this rule of pale urine during your waking hours is a good indicator that you are well hydrated. Medications, vitamins, and certain foods may alter urine color despite adequate hydration. Due to the varying levels of physical and vocal activity of many performers, in order to maintain adequate oral hydration, the use of a hydration calculator based on activity level may be a better choice. These hydration calculators are easily accessible online and take into account the amount and level of activity the performer engages in on a daily basis. In a recent study of the vocal habits of music theater performers, one of the findings indicated a significantly underhydrated group of performers (Donahue, LeBorgne, Brehm, Weinrich, in review).

Laryngeal and pharyngeal dryness as well as "thick, sticky, mucus" are often complaints of singers. Combating these concerns and maintaining an adequate viscosity of mucus for performance has resulted in some research. As a reminder of laryngeal and swallowing anatomy, nothing that is swallowed (or gargled) goes over or touches the vocal folds directly (or one would choke). Therefore, nothing that a singer eats or drinks ever touches the vocal folds, and in order to adequately hydrate the mucus membranes of the vocal folds, one must consume enough fluids for the body to produce a thin mucus. Therefore, any "vocal" effects from swallowed products are limited to potential pharyngeal and oral changes, not the vocal folds themselves.

The effects of systemic hydration are well documented in the literature. There is evidence to suggest that adequate hydration will provide some protection of the laryngeal mucosal membranes when they are placed under increased collision forces as well as reducing the amount of effort (phonation threshold pressure) to produce voice (Leydon, Sivasankar, Falciglia, Atkins, & Fisher 2009; Leydon, Wroblewski, Eichorn, & Sivasankar 2010; Sivasankar & Leydon 2010; Yiu & Chan 2003). This is important for the singer because it means that with adequate hydration and consistency of mucus, the effort to produce voice is less and that your vocal folds are better protected from injury. Imagine the friction and heat produced when two dry hands rub together and then what happens if you put lotion on your hands. The mechanisms in the larynx to provide appropriate mucus production are not fully understood, but there is enough evidence at this time to support oral hydration as a vital component of every singer's vocal health regime to maintain appropriate mucosal viscosity.

Although very rare, overhydration (hyperhidrosis) can result in dehydration and even illness or death. An overindulgence of fluids essentially makes the kidneys work "overtime" and flushes too much water out of the body. This excessive fluid loss in a rapid manner can be detrimental to the body.

In addition to drinking water to systemically monitor hydration, there are many nonregulated products on the market for performers that lay claim to improving the laryngeal environment (e.g., Entertainer's Secret, Throat Coat Tea, Greathers Pastilles, Slippery Elm, etc.). Although there may be little detriment in using these products, quantitative research documenting change in laryngeal mucosa is sparse (Brinckmann, Sigwart, & vanHouten Taylor 2003; Roy, Tanner, Gray, Blomgren, & Fisher 2003). One study suggests that the use of Throat Coat when compared to a placebo treatment for pharyngitis did show a significant difference in decreasing the perception of sore throat. Another study compared the use of Entertainer's Secret to two other nebulized agents and its effect on phonation threshold pressure (PTP). There was no positive benefit in decreasing PTP with Entertainer's Secret.

Many singers use personal steam inhalers and/or room humidification to supplement oral hydration and aid in combating laryngeal dryness. There are several considerations for singers who choose to use external means of adding moisture to the air they breathe. Personal steam inhalers are portable and can often be used backstage or in the hotel room for the traveling performer. Typically, water is placed in the steamer and the face is placed over the steam for inhalation. Because the mucus membranes of the larynx are composed of a saltwater solution, one study looked at the use of nebulized saline in comparison to plain water and its potential effects on effort or ease to sound production in classically trained sopranos (Tanner, Roy, Merrill, Muntz, Houtz, Sauder, Elstad, & Wright-Costa 2010). Data suggested that perceived effort to produce voice was less in the saline group than the plain-water group. This indicated that the singers who used the saltwater solution reported less effort to sing after breathing in the saltwater than singers who used plain water. It was hypothesized by the researchers that because the body's mucus is not plain water (rather it is a saltwater—think about your tears), when you use plain water for steam inhalation, it may actually draw the salt from your own saliva, resulting in a dehydrating effect.

In addition to personal steamers, other options for air humidification come in varying sizes of humidifiers from room size to whole house humidifiers. When choosing between a warm air or cool mist humidifier considerations include both personal preference and needs. One of the primary reasons warm mist humidifiers are not recommended for young children is due to the risk of burns from the heating element. Both the warm mist and cool air humidifiers act similarly in adding moisture to the environmental air. External air humidification may be beneficial and provide a level of comfort for many singers. Regular cleaning of the humidifier is vital to prevent bacteria and mold buildup. Also, depending on the hardness of the water, it is important to avoid mineral buildup on the device and distilled water may be recommended for some humidifiers.

For traveling performers who often stay in hotels, fly on airplanes, or are generally exposed to other dry-air environments, there are products on the market designed to help minimize drying effects. One such device is called Humidflyer, which is a facemask (www.humidiflyer.com/) designed with a filter to recycle the moisture of a person's own breath and replenish moisture on each breath cycle.

For dry nasal passages or to clear sinuses, many singers use Neti pots. Many singers use this homeopathic flushing of the nasal passages regularly. Research supports the use of a Neti pot as a part of allergy relief and chronic rhinosinusitis control when utilized properly, sometimes in combination with medical management (Brown & Grahm 2004; Dunn, Dion, & McMains 2013). Conversely, long-term use of nasal irrigation (without taking intermittent breaks from daily use) may result in washing out the "good" mucus of the nasal passages, which naturally help to rid the nose of infections. A study presented at the American College of Allergy, Asthma & Immunology (ACAAI) 2009 Annual Scientific Meeting reported that when a group of individuals who were using twice daily nasal irrigation for one year discontinued using it, they had an increase in acute rhinosinusitits (Nsouli 2009).

Tea, Honey, and Gargle to Keep the Throat Healthy

Regarding the use of general teas (which many singers combine with honey or lemon), there is likely no harm in the use of decaffeinated tea (caffeine may cause systemic dryness). The warmth of the tea may provide a soothing sensation to the pharynx and the act of swallowing can be relaxing for the muscles of the throat. Honey has shown promising results as an effective cough suppressant in the pediatric population (Shadkam, Mozaffari-Khosravi, & Mozayan 2010). The dose of honey given to the children in the study was two teaspoons. Gargling with salt or apple cider vinegar and water are also popular home remedies for many singers with the uses being from soothing the throat to curing reflux. Gargling plain water has been shown to be efficacious in reducing the risk of contracting upper respiratory infections (Satomura, Kitamura, Kawamura, Shimbo, Watanabe, Kamei, Takana, & Tamakoshi 2005). I suggest that when gargling, the singer only "bubble" the water with air and avoid engaging the vocal folds in sound production. Saltwater as a gargle has long been touted as a sore throat remedy and can be traced back to 2700 BCE in China for treating gum disease (health.howstuffworks.com/wellness/oral-care/products/saltwater-as-mouthwash.htm). The science behind a saltwater rinse for everything from oral hygiene to sore throat is that salt (sodium chloride) may act as a natural analgesic (pain killer) and may also kill bacteria. Similar to the effects that not enough salt in the water may have on drawing the salt out of the tissue in the steam inhalation, if you oversaturate the water solution with excess salt and gargle it, it may act to draw water out of the oral mucosa, thus reducing inflammation.

Another popular home remedy reported by singers is the use of apple cider vinegar to help with everything from acid reflux to sore throats. Dating back to 3300 BCE, apple cider vinegar was reported as a medicinal remedy, and it became popular in the 1970s as a weight loss diet cocktail. Popular media reports apple cider vinegar can improve conditions from acne and arthritis to nosebleeds and varicose veins (www.healthline.com/natstandardcontent/apple-cider-vinegar). Specific efficacy data regarding the beneficial nature of apple cider vinegar for the purpose of sore throat, pharyngeal inflammation, and/or reflux has not been reported in the literature at this time. Of the peer-reviewed studies found in the literature, one discussed possible esophageal erosion and inconsistency of actual product in tablet form (Hill, Woodruff, Foote, & Barreto-Alcoba 2005). Therefore, at this time, strong evidence supporting the use of apple cider vinegar is not published.

Medications and the Voice

Medications (over the counter, prescription, and herbal) may have resultant drying effects on the body and often the laryngeal mucosa.

General classes of drugs with potential drying effects include: antidepressants, antihypertensives, diuretics, ADD/ADHD medications, some oral acne medications, hormones, allergy drugs, and vitamin C in high doses. The National Center for Voice and Speech (NCVS) provides a listing of some common medications with potential voice side effects including laryngeal dryness. This listing does not take into account all medications, so singers should always ask their pharmacist of the potential side effects of a given medication. Due to the significant number of drugs on the market, it is safe to say that most pharmacists will not be acutely aware of "vocal side effects," but if dryness is listed as a potential side effect of the drug, you may assume that all body systems could be affected. Under no circumstances should you stop taking a prescribed medication without consulting your physician first. As every person has a different body chemistry and reaction to medication, just because a medication lists dryness as a potential side effect, it does not necessarily mean you will experience that side effect. Conversely, if you begin a new medication and notice physical or vocal changes that are unexpected, you should consult with your physician. Ultimately, the goal of medical management for any condition is to achieve the most benefits with the least side effects. A list of possible resources for singers regarding prescription drugs and herbs are found online at:

- www.fda.gov/OHRMS/DOCKETS/98FR/06D-0480-GLD0001. PDF
- nccam.nih.gov/health/herbsataglance.htm
- www.nlm.nih.gov/medlineplus/druginfo/herb_All.html
- www.ncvs.org

In contrast to medications that tend to dry, there are medications formulated to increase saliva production or alter the viscosity of mucus. Medically, these drugs are often used to treat patients who have had a loss of saliva production due to surgery or radiation. Mucalitic agents are used to thin secretions as needed. As a singer if you feel that you need to use a mucalitic agent on a consistent basis, it may be worth considering getting to the root of the laryngeal dryness symptom and seeking a professional option by an otolaryngologist.

Reflux and the Voice

Gastroesophageal reflux (GERD) and/or laryngopharyngeal reflux (LPR) can have a devastating impact on the singer if not recognized and treated appropriately. Although GERD and LPR are related, they are considered as slightly different diseases. GERD (Latin root meaning "flowing back") is the reflux of digestive enzymes, acids, and other stomach contents into the esophagus (food pipe). If this backflow is propelled through the upper esophagus and into the throat (larynx and pharynx), it is referred to as LPR. It is not uncommon to have both GERD and LPR, but they can occur independently.

More frequently, people with GERD have decreased esophageal clearing. Esophagitis, or inflammation of the esophagus, is also associated with GERD. People with GERD often feel heartburn. LPR symptoms are often "silent" and do not include heartburn. Specific symptoms of LPR may include some or all of the following: lump in the throat sensation, feeling of constant need to clear the throat/post nasal drip, longer vocal warm-up time, quicker vocal fatigue, loss of high frequency range, worse voice in the morning, sore throat, and bitter/raw/brackish taste in the mouth. If you experience these symptoms on a regular basis, it is advised that you consider a medical consultation for your symptoms. Prolonged, untreated GERD or LPR can lead to permanent changes in the esophagus and/or larynx. Untreated LPR also provides a laryngeal environment that is conducive for vocal fold lesions to occur as it inhibits normal healing mechanisms.

Treatment of LPR and GERD generally include both dietary and lifestyle modifications in addition to medical management. Some of the dietary recommendations include: elimination of caffeinated and carbonated beverages, smoking cessation, no alcohol use, and limiting tomatoes, acidic foods and drinks, and raw onions or peppers, to name a few. Also, avoidance of high-fat foods is recommended. From a lifestyle perspective, suggested changes include: not eating within three hours of lying down, eating small meals frequently (instead of large meals), elevating the head of your bead, avoiding tight clothing around the belly, and not bending over or exercising too soon after you eat.

Reflux medications fall in three general categories: antacids, H2 blockers, and proton pump inhibitors (PPI). There are now combination drugs that include both an H2 blocker and proton pump inhibitor. Every medication has both associated risks and benefits, and singers should be aware of the possible benefits and side effects of the medications they take. In general terms, antacids (e.g., Tums, Mylanta, Gaviscon) neutralize stomach acid. H2 (histamine blockers) such as Axid (nizatidine), Tagamet (cimetidine), Pepcid (famotidine), and Zantac (ranitidine), work to decrease acid production in the stomach by preventing histamine from triggering the H2 receptors to produce more acid. Then there are the PPIs: Nexium (esomeprazole), Prevacid (lansoprazole), Protonix (pantoprazole), AcipHex (rabeprazole), Prilosec (omeprazole), and Dexilant (dexlansoprazole). PPIs act as a last line of defense to decrease acid production by blocking the last step in gastric juice secretion. Some of the most recent drugs to combat GERD/LPR are combination drugs (e.g., Zegrid [sodium bicarbonate plus omeprazole]) that provide a short-acting response (sodium bicarbonate) and a long release (omeprazole). Because some singers prefer a holistic approach to reflux management, strict dietary and lifestyle compliance is recommended and consultation with both your primary care physician and naturopath are warranted in that situation. Efficacy data on nonregulated herbs, vitamins, and supplements is limited, but some data does exist.

Physical Exercise

Vocal athletes, like other physical athletes, should consider how and what they do to maintain both cardiovascular fitness and muscular strength. In today's performance culture, it is rare that a performer stands still and sings, unless in a recital or choral setting. The range of physical activity can vary from light movement to high-intensity choreography with acrobatics. As performers are being required to increase their on-stage physical activity level from the operatic stage to the pop-star arena, overall physical fitness is imperative to avoid compromise in the vocal system. Breathlessness will result in compensation by the larynx, which is now attempting to regulate the air. Compensatory vocal behaviors over time may result in a change in vocal performance. The health benefits of both cardiovascular training and strength training are well documented in the literature for physical athletes, but relatively rare for vocal performers.

Mental Wellness

Vocal performers must maintain a mental focus during performance and a mental toughness during auditioning and training. Rarely during vocal performance training programs is this important aspect of performance addressed, and it is often left to the individual performer to develop their own strategy or coping mechanism. Yet, many performers are on antianxiety or antidepressant drugs (which may be the direct result of performance-related issues). If the sports world is again used as a parallel for mental toughness, there are no elite-level athletes (and few junior-level athletes) who don't utilize the services of a performance/sports psychologist to maximize focus and performance. I recommend that performers consider the potential benefits of a performance psychologist to help maximize vocal performance. Several references that may be of interest to the singer include: Joanna Cazden's *Visualization for Singers* and Shirlee Emmons and Alma Thomas's *Power Performance for Singers: Transcending the Barriers.*

Unlike instrumentalists, whose performance is dependent on accurate playing of an external musical instrument, the singer's instrument is uniquely intact and subject to the emotional confines of the brain and body in which it is housed. Musical performance anxiety (MPA) can be career threatening for all musicians, but perhaps the vocal athlete is more severely impacted (Spahn, Echternach, Zander, Voltmer, & Richter 2010). The majority of literature on MPA is dedicated to instrumentalists, but the basis of definition, performance effects, and treatment options can be considered for vocal athletes (Anderson 2011; Arneson 2010; Brantigan, Brantigan, & Joseph 1982; Brugues 2011; Chanel 1992; Corby, undated; Drinkwater & Klopper 2010; Fehm & Schmidt 2006; Fredrikson & Gunnarsson 1992; Gates, Saegert, Wilson, Johnson, Shepherd, & Hearne 1985; Gates & Montalbo 1987; Kenny, Davis, & Oates 2004; Khalsa, Shorter, Cope, Wyshak, & Sklar 2009; Lazarus & Abramovitz 2004; Markovska-Simoska, McGinnis, & Milling 2005; Pop-Jordanova & Georgiev 2008; Nagel 2010; Neftel, Adler, Käppeli, Rossi, Dolder, Käser, Bruggesser, & Vorkauf 1982; Powell 2004; Schneider & Chesky 2011; Spahn et al. 2010; Studer, Danuser, Hildebrandt, Arial, & Gomez 2011; Studer, Gomez, Hildebrandt, Arial, & Danuser 2011; Taborsky 2007; van Kemenade, van Son, & van Heesch 1995; Walker & Nordin-Bates 2010; Wesner, Noyes, & Davis; 1990).

Fear is a natural reaction to a stressful situation, and there is a fine line between emotional excitation and perceived threat (real or imagined). The job of a performer is to convey to an audience through vocal production, physical gestures, and facial expression a most heightened state of emotion. Otherwise, why would audience members pay top dollar to sit for two or three hours for a mundane experience? Not only is there the emotional conveyance of the performance, but also the internal turmoil often experienced by the singers themselves in preparation for elite performance. It is well documented in the literature that even the most elite performers have experienced debilitating performance anxiety. MPA is defined on a continuum with anxiety levels ranging from low to high and has been reported to comprise four distinct components: affect, cognition, behavior, and physiology (Spahn et al. 2010). Affect comprises feelings (e.g., doom, panic, anxiety). Effected cognition will result in altered levels of concentration, while the behavior component results in postural shifts, quivering, and trembling. Finally physiologically the body's autonomic nervous system (ANS) will activate, resulting in the "fight or flight" response.

In recent years, researchers have been able to define two distinct neurological pathways for MPA. The first pathway happens quickly and without conscious input (ANS) resulting in the same fear stimulus as if a person were put into an emergent, life-threatening situation. In those situations, the brain releases adrenaline, resulting in physical changes of: increased heart rate, increased respiration, shaking, pale skin, dilated pupils, slowed digestion, bladder relaxation, dry mouth, and dry eyes, all of which severely affect vocal performance. The second pathway that has been identified results in a conscious identification of the fear/threat and a much slower physiologic response. With the second neuromotor response, the performer has a chance to recognize the fear, process how to deal with the fear, and respond accordingly.

Treatment modalities to address MPA include psycho-behavioral therapy (including biofeedback) and drug therapies. Elite physical performance athletes have been shown to benefit from visualization techniques and psychological readiness training, yet within the performing arts community, stage fright may be considered a weakness or character flaw precluding readiness for professional performance. On the contrary, vocal athletes, like physical athletes, should mentally prepare themselves for optimal competition (auditions) and performance. Learning to convey emotion without eliciting an internal emotional response by the vocal athlete may take the skill of an experienced psychologist to help change ingrained neural pathways. Ultimately, control and understanding of MPA will enhance performance and prepare the vocal athlete for the most intense performance demands without vocal compromise.

VOCAL WELLNESS: INJURY PREVENTION

In order to prevent vocal injury and understand vocal wellness in the singer, general knowledge of common causes of voice disorders is imperative. One common cause of voice disorders is vocally abusive behaviors or misuse of the voice to include phonotraumatic behaviors such as yelling, screaming, loud talking, talking over noise, throat clearing, coughing, harsh sneezing, and boisterous laughing. Chronic or less than optimal vocal properties such as poor breathing techniques, inappropriate phonatory habits during conversational speech (glottal fry, hard glottal attacks), inapt pitch, loudness, rate of speech, and/or hyperfunctional laryngeal area muscle tone may also negatively impact vocal function. Medically related etiologies, which also have the potential to impact vocal function, range from untreated chronic allergies and sinusitis to endocrine dysfunction and hormonal imbalance. Direct trauma, such as a blow to the neck or the risk of vocal fold damage during intubation, can impact optimal performance in vocal athletes depending on the nature and extent of the trauma. Finally, external irritants ranging from cigarette smoke to reflux directly impact the laryngeal mucosa and ultimately can lead to laryngeal pathology.

Vocal hygiene education and compliance may be one of the primary essential components for maintaining the voice throughout a career (Behrman, Rutledge, Hembree, & Sheridan 2008). This section will provide the singer with information on prevention of vocal injury. However, just like a professional sports athlete, it is unlikely that a professional vocal athlete will go through an entire career without some compromise in vocal function. This may be a common upper respiratory infection that creates vocal fold swelling for a short time, or it may be a "vocal accident" that is career threatening. Regardless, the knowledge of how to take care of your voice is essential for any vocal athlete.

Train Like an Athlete for Vocal Longevity

Performers seek instant gratification in performance sometimes at the cost of gradual vocal building for a lifetime of healthy singing. Historically, vocal pedagogues required their students to perform vocalises exclusively for up to two years before beginning any song literature. Singers gradually built their voice by ingraining appropriate muscle memory and neuromotor patterns through development of aesthetically pleasing tones, onsets, breath management, and support. There was an intensive master-apprentice relationship and rigorous vocal guidelines to maintain a place within a given studio. Time off was taken if a vocal injury ensued or careers potentially were ended, and students were asked to leave a given singing studio if their voice was unable to withstand the rigors of training. Training vocal athletes today has evolved and appears driven to create a "product" quickly, perhaps at the expense of the longevity of the singer. Pop stars emerging well before puberty are doing international concert tours, yet many young artist programs in the classical arena do not consider singers for their programs until they are in their mid- to late twenties.

Each vocal genre presents with different standards and vocal demands. Therefore, the amount and degree of vocal training are varied. Some would argue that performing extensively without adequate vocal training and development is ill-advised, yet singers today are thrust onto the stage at very young ages. Dancers, instrumentalists, and physical athletes all spend many hours per day developing muscle strength, memory, and proper technique for their craft. The more advanced the artist or athlete, generally the more specific the training protocol becomes. Consideration of training vocal athletes in this same fashion is recommended. One would generally not begin a young, inexperienced singer without previous vocal training on a Wagner aria. Similarly, in nonclassical vocal music, there are easy, moderate, and difficult pieces to consider pending level of vocal development and training.

Basic pedagogical training of alignment, breathing, voice production, and resonance are essential building blocks for development of good voice production. Muscle memory and development of appropriate muscle patterns happens slowly over time with appropriate repetitive practice. Doing too much, too soon for any athlete (physical or vocal) will result in an increased risk for injury. When the singer is being asked to do "vocal gymnastics," they must be sure to have a solid basis of strength and stamina in the appropriate muscle groups to perform consistently with minimal risk of injury.

Vocal Fitness Program

One generally does not get out of bed first thing in the morning and try to do a split. Yet many singers go directly into a practice session or audition without proper warm-up. Think of your larynx like your knee, made up of cartilages, ligaments, and muscles. Vocal health is dependent upon appropriate warm-ups (to get things moving), drills for technique, and then cool-downs (at the end of your day). Consider vocal warm-ups a "gentle stretch." Depending on the needs of the singer, warm-ups should include physical stretching; postural alignment self-checks; breathing exercises to promote rib cage, abdominal, and back expansion; vocal stretches (glides up to stretch the vocal folds and glides down to contract the vocal folds); articulatory stretches (yawning, facial stretches); and mental warm-ups (to provide focus for the task at hand). Vocalises, in my opinion, are designed as exercises to go beyond warm-ups and prepare the body and voice for the technical and vocal challenges of the music they sing. They are varied and address the technical level and genre of the singer to maximize performance and vocal growth. Cool-downs are a part of most athletes' workouts. However, singers often do not use cool-downs (physical, mental, and vocal) at the end of a performance. A recent study looked specifically at the benefits of vocal cool-downs in singers and found that singers who used a vocal cool-down had decreased effort to produce voice the next day (Gottliebson 2011).

Systemic hydration as a means to keep the vocal folds adequately lubricated for the amount of impact and friction that they will undergo has been previously discussed in this chapter. Compliance with adequate oral hydration recommendations is important and subsequently so is the minimization of agents that could potentially dry the membranes (e.g., caffeine, medications, dry air). The body produces approximately two quarts of mucus per day. If not adequately hydrated, the mucus tends to be thick and sticky. Poor hydration is similar to not putting enough oil in the car engine. Frankly, if the gears do not work as well, there is increased friction and heat, and the engine is not efficient.

Speak Well, Sing Well

Optimize the speaking voice utilizing ideal frequency range, breath, intensity, rate, and resonance. Singers generally are vocally enthusiastic individuals who talk a lot and often talk loudly. During typical conversation, the average fundamental speaking frequency (times per second the vocal folds are impacting) for a male varies from 100 to 150Hz and 180 to 230Hz for women. Because of the delicate structure of the vocal folds and the importance of the layered microstructure vibrating efficiently and effectively to produce voice, vocal behaviors or outside factors that compromise the integrity of the vibration patterns of the vocal folds may be considered phonotrauma.

Phonotraumatic behaviors can include yelling, screaming, loud talking, harsh sneezing, and harsh laughing. Elimination of phontraumatic behaviors is essential for good vocal health. The louder one speaks, the farther apart the vocal folds move from midline, the harder they impact, and the longer they stay closed. A tangible example would be to take your hands, move them only six inches apart and clap as hard and as loudly as you can for ten seconds. Now, move your hands two feet apart and clap as hard, loudly, and quickly as possible for ten seconds. The farther apart your hands are, the more air you move and the louder the clap, and the skin on the hands becomes red and ultimately swollen (if you do it long enough and hard enough). This is what happens to the vocal folds with repeated impact at increased vocal intensities. The vocal folds are approximately 17mm in length and vibrate at 220 times per second on A3, 440 on A4, 880 on A5, and more than 1,000 per second when singing a high C. That is a lot of impact for little muscles. Consider this fact when singing loudly or in a high tessitura for prolonged periods of time. It becomes easy to see why women are more prone than men to laryngeal impact injuries due to the frequency range of the voice alone.

In addition to the amount of cycles per second the vocal folds are impacting, singers need to be aware of their vocal intensity (volume).

Check the volume of the speaking and singing voice and for conversational speech and consider using a distance of three to five feet as a gauge for how loud you need to be in general conversation (about an arm's-length distance). Cell phones and speaking on a Bluetooth device in a car generally results in louder than conversational vocal intensity, and singers are advised to minimize unnecessary use of these devices.

Singers should be encouraged to take "vocal naps" during their day. A vocal nap would be a short period of time (five minutes to an hour) of complete silence. Although the vocal folds are rarely completely still (because they move when you swallow and breathe), a vocal nap minimizes impact and vibration for a short window of time. A physical nap can also be refreshing for the singer mentally and physically.

Avoid Environmental Irritants: Alcohol, Smoking, Drugs

Arming singers with information on the actual effects of environmental irritants so that they can make informed choices on engaging in exposure to these potential toxins is essential. The glamor that continues to be associated with smoking, drinking, and drugs can be tempered with the deaths of popular stars such as Amy Winehouse and Cory Monteith who engaged in life-ending choices. There is extensive documentation about the long-term effects of toxic and carcinogenic substances, but here are a few key facts to consider when choosing whether to partake.

Alcohol, although it does not go over the vocal folds directly, does have a systemic drying effect. Due to the acidity in alcohol, it may increase the likelihood of reflux, resulting in hoarseness and other laryngeal pathologies. Consuming alcohol generally decreases one's inhibitions and therefore you are more likely to sing and do things that you would not typically do under the influence of alcohol.

Beyond the carcinogens in nicotine and tobacco, the heat at which a cigarette burns is well above the boiling temperature of water (water boils at 212°F; cigarettes burn at over 1400°F). No one would consider pouring a pot of boiling water on their hand, and yet the burning temperature for a cigarette results in significant heat over the oral mucosa and vocal folds. The heat alone can create deterioration in the lining, resulting in polypoid degeneration. Obviously, cigarette smoking has been well documented as a cause for laryngeal cancer.

Marijuana and other street drugs are not only addictive, but can cause permanent mucosal lining changes depending on the drug used and the method of delivery. If you or one of your singer colleagues is experiencing a drug or alcohol problem, provide them with information and support on getting appropriate counseling and help.

SMART PRACTICE STRATEGIES FOR SKILL DEVELOPMENT AND VOICE CONSERVATION

Daily practice and drills for skill acquisition are an important part of any singer's training. However, overpracticing or inefficient practicing may be detrimental to the voice. Consider practice sessions of athletes: they may practice four to eight hours per day broken into one- to two-hour training sessions with a period of rest and recovery in between sessions. Although we cannot parallel the sports model without adequate evidence in the vocal athlete, the premise of short, intense, focused practice sessions is logical for the singer. Similar to physical exercise, it is suggested that practice sessions do not have to be all "singing." Rather, structuring sessions so that one-third of the session is spent on warm-up; one-third on vocalise, text work, rhythms, character development, and so on; and one-third on repertoire will allow the singer to function in a more efficient vocal manner. Building the amount of time per practice session—increasing duration by five minutes per week, building to sixty to ninety minutes—may be effective (e.g., Week 1: 20 minutes 3x per day; Week 2: 25 minutes 3x per day, etc.).

Vary the "vocal workout" during your week. For example, if you do the same physical exercise in the same way day after day with the same intensity and pattern, you will likely experience repetitive strain-type injuries. However, cross-training or varying the type and level of exercise aids in injury prevention. So when planning your practice sessions for a given week (or rehearsal process for a given role), consider varying your vocal intensity, tessitura, and exercises to maximize your training sessions, building stamina, muscle memory, and skill acquisition. For example, one day you may spend more time on learning rhythms and translation and the next day you spend thirty minutes performing coloratura exercises to prepare for a specific role. Take one day a week off from vocal training and give your voice a break. This does not mean complete vocal rest (although some singers find this beneficial), but rather a day without singing and limited talking.

Practice Your Mental Focus

Mental wellness and stress management are equally as important as vocal training for vocal athletes. Addressing any mental health issues is paramount to developing the vocal artist. This may include anything from daily mental exercises/meditation/focus to overcoming performance anxiety to more serious mental health issues/illness. Every person can benefit from improved focus and mental acuity.

SPECIFIC VOCAL WELLNESS CONCERNS FOR THE VOCAL JAZZ ARTIST

Vocal jazz artists evolved in the early 1900s, and the output of these singers required that they make their voices emulate the instruments in terms of timbre, articulation, quality, and range. Jazz singing is as much about the ability to improvise, incorporate an appropriate mood, and convey the unique musical genius of the artists creating the music as it is about "vocal beauty" or "vocal health." Not everything about a jazz voice is necessarily what would be considered by other vocal standards as healthy, but most jazz vocal artists are unique in their sound and the soulful production and use of their instrument. Vocal jazz has evolved and includes an acceptable variety of qualities that may or may not be aesthetically acceptable in other styles of singing. Many of the early well-known jazz singers had little formal vocal training, yet they were able to connect with their audience on a visceral level with their voices.

Literature related to the vocal health, habits, and hygiene is limited in jazz singers (Tolson & Cuyjet 2007; Singer & Mirhej 2006; Pinheiro & Dowd 2009). Much of the literature discusses the use of drugs (in early jazz musicians—not specifically singers) and the psychosocial aspects of their lives.

Physical Fitness

Unlike musical theater, rock and roll, or contemporary pop, many jazz artists are not required to put on high physical intensity shows. That does not mean that these performers don't use a high amount of energy when they perform, but rather that the concert/show/performance is more about the vocal and instrumental experience than a performance "spectacle." General physical health guidelines should hold true for jazz vocalists, as they should be both physically and vocally in shape necessary to their performance demands.

Healthy Singing

Vocal jazz requires that the singer have a flexible, agile, dynamic instrument with appropriate stamina. Jazz singers must have a good command of their instrument as well as exceptional underlying intention to what they are singing, as it is much more about feeling and intent resulting in an appropriate acoustic output. The creative and performance environments for jazz singers can be less than optimal from a vocal health perspective (e.g., smoky bars, substance abuse during creative endeavors). Aside from the tips listed above regarding smoking, alcohol, and substance use, when having to perform in smoky environments, here are two additional considerations. First, if the singer takes a spray bottle (such as an empty/washed-out window cleaner bottle) and fills it with water, you can spritz the air on the stage prior to performance and in between sets to pull the dust to the floor (the water particles will weigh down the dust and pull to the floor and out of your face). Secondly, the use of a small fan that blows the air toward the audience will draw smoky air in from the stage and away from the singer (back toward the audience). Depending on your stage setup, this fan can either be placed at the singer's feet or on speakers. Multiple fans are fine.

Jazz vocalists use microphones and amplification. Amplification for the jazz performer can be used to maximize vocal health by allowing the singer to produce voice in an efficient manner while the sound engineer is effectively able to mix, amplify, and add effects to the voice. Understanding both the utility and limits of a given microphone and sound system is essential for the jazz artist both for live and studio performances. Using an appropriate microphone not only can enhance the jazz singer's performance but can reduce vocal load for the singer. Emotional extremes (intimacy and exultation) can be enhanced by appropriate microphone choice, placement, and acoustical mixing, thus saving the singer's voice.

Not everything a jazz singer does is "vocally healthy," sometimes because the emotional expression may be so intense it results in vocal collision forces that are extreme. Even if the jazz singer does not have formal vocal training, cross-training the instrument (which can mean singing in both high and low registers with varying intensities and resonance options) before and after practice sessions is likely a vital component to minimizing vocal injury. Ultimately, the singer must learn to provide the most output with the least "cost" to the system. Taking care of the physical instrument through daily physical exercise, adequate nutrition and hydration, and maintaining focused attention on performance will provide a necessary basis for vocal health during performance. Small doses of high-intensity singing (or speaking) will limit impact stress on the vocal folds. Finally, attention to the mind, body, and voice will provide the singer with an awareness when something is wrong. This awareness and knowledge of when to rest or seek help will promote vocal well-being for the singer throughout his or her career.

BIBLIOGRAPHY

Behrman, A., Rutledge, J., Hembree, A., & Sheridan, S. (2008). Vocal hygiene education, voice production therapy, and the role of patient adherence: A treatment effectiveness study in women with phonotrauma. *Journal of Speech, Language, and Hearing Research, 51,* 350–366.

Brinckmann, J., Sigwart, H., & vanHouten Taylor, L. (2003). Safety and efficacy of a traditional herbal medicine (Throat Coat) in symptomatic temporary relief of pain in patients with acute pharyngitis: a multicenter, prospective, randomized, double-blinded, placebo-controlled study. *Journal of Alternative and Complementary Medicine, 9*(2), 285–298, www.ncbi.nlm.nih.gov/pubmed/?term=Throat+coat+tea.

Brown, C., & Grahm, S. (2004). Nasal irrigations: good or bad? *Current Opinion in Otolaryngology, Head and Neck Surgery, 12*(1), 9–13.

Dunn, J., Dion, G., & McMains, K. (2013). Efficacy of nasal symptom relief. *Current Opinion in Otolaryngology, Head and Neck Surgery, 21*(3), 248–251.

Elias, M. E., Sataloff, R. T., Rosen, D. C., Heuer, R. J., & Spiegel, J. R. (1997). Normal strobovideolaryngoscopy: variability in healthy singers. *Journal of Voice, 11*(1), 104–107.

Evans, R. W., Evans, R. I., & Carvajal, S. (1998). Survey of injuries among west end performers. *Occupational and Environmental Medicine, 55,* 585–593.

Evans, R. W., Evans, R. I., Carvajal, S., & Perry, S. (1996). A survey of injuries among Broadway performers. *Am J Public Health, 86,* 77.

Gottliebson, R. O. (2011). The efficacy of cool-down exercises in the practice regimen of elite singers. Dissertation, University of Cincinnati.

Heman-Ackah, Y., Dean, C., & Sataloff, R. T. (2002). Strobovideolaryngoscopic findings in singing teachers. *Journal of Voice, 16*(1), 81–86.

Hill, L., Woodruff, L., Foote, J., & Barreto-Alcoba, M. (2005). Esophageal injury by apple cider vinegar tablets and subsequent evaluation of products. *Journal of the American Dietetics Association, 105*(7), 1141–1144.

Hoffman-Ruddy, B., Lehman, J., Crandell, C., Ingram, D., & Sapienza, C. (2001). Laryngostroboscopic, acoustic, and environmental characteristics of high-risk vocal performers. *Journal of Voice, 15*(4), 543–552.

Korovin, G., & LeBorgne, W. (2009). A longitudinal examination of potential vocal injury in musical theater performers. The Voice Foundation's 36th Annual Symposium: Care of the Professional Voice, June 3–7, Philadelphia.

Koufman, J. A., Radomski, T. A., Joharji, G. M., Russell, G. B., & Pillsbury, D. C. (1996). Laryngealbiomechanics of the singing voice. *Otolaryngol Head Neck Surgery, 115,* 527–537.

LeBorgne, W. (2001). Defining the belt voice: Perceptual judgments and objective measures. Dissertation, University of Cincinnati.

LeBorgne, W., Donahue, E., Brehm, S., & Weinrich, B. (2012). Prevalence of vocal pathology in incoming freshman musical theatre majors: A 10-year retrospective study. Fall Voice Conference, October 4–6, New York City.

Leydon, C., Sivasankar, M., Falciglia, D., Atkins, C., & Fisher, K. (2009). Vocal fold surface hydration: A review. *Journal of Voice, 23*(6), 658–665.

Leydon, C., Wroblewski, M., Eichorn, N., & Sivasankar, M. (2010). A meta-analysis of outcomes of hydration intervention on phonation threshold pressure. *Journal of Voice, 24*(6), 637–643.

Lundy, D., Casiano, R., Sullivan, P., Roy, S., Xue, J., & Evans, J. (1999). Incidence of abnormal laryngeal findings in asymptomatic singing students. *Otolaryngology—Head and Neck Surgery, 121,* 69–77.

Nsouli, T. (2009). Long-term use of nasal saline irrigation: harmful or helpful? American College of Allergy, Asthma & Immunology (ACAAI) 2009 Annual Scientific Meeting: Abstract 32, presented November 8.

Phyland, D.J., Oates, J., & Greenwood, K. (1999). Self-reported voice problems among three groups of professional singers. *Journal of Voice, 13,* 602–611.

Pinheiro, D., & Dowd, T. (2009). All that jazz: The success of jazz musicians in three metropolitan areas. *Poetics, 37,* 490–506.

Roy, N., Tanner, K., Gray, S., Blomgren, M., & Fisher, K. (2003). An evaluation of the effects of three laryngeal lubricants on phonation threshold pressure (PTP). *Journal of Voice, 17*(3), 331–342, www.ncbi.nlm.nih.gov/pubmed/?term=Entertainer%E2%80%99s+Secret.

Satomura, K. Kitamura, T., Kawamura, T., Shimbo, T., Watanabe, M., Kamei, M., Takana, Y., & Tamakoshi, A. (2005). Prevention of upper respiratory tract infections by gargling: A randomized trial. *American Journal of Preventative Medicine, 29*(4), 302–307.

Shadkam, M., Mozaffari-Khosravi, H., & Mozayan, M. (2010). A comparison of the effect of honey, dextromethorphan, and diphenhydramine on nightly cough and sleep quality in children and their parents. *Journal of Alternative and Complementary Medicine, 16*(7), 787–793.

Singer, M., & Mirhej, G. (2006). High notes: The role of drugs in the making of jazz. *Journal of Ethnicity in Substance Abuse, 5*(4), 1–39.

Sivasankar, M., & Leydon, C. (2010). The role of hydration in vocal fold physiology. *Current Opinion in Otolaryngology Head & Neck Surgery, 18*(3), 171–175.

Tanner, K., Roy, N., Merrill, R., Muntz, F., Houtz, D., Sauder, C., Elstad, M., & Wright-Costa, J. (2010). Nebulized isotonic saline versus water following a laryngeal desiccation challenge in classically trained sopranos. *Journal of Speech Language and Hearing Research, 53*(6), 1555–1566.

Tepe, E. S., Deutsch, E. S., Sampson, Q., Lawless, S., Reilly, J. S., & Sataloff, R. T. (2002). A pilot survey of vocal health in young singers. *J Voice, 16,* 244–247.

Tolson, G., & Cuyjet, M. (2007). Jazz and substance abuse: Road to creative genius or pathway to premature death. *International Journal of Law and Psychiatry, 30,* 530–538.

Yang, J., Tibbetts, A., Covassin, T., Cheng, G., Nayar, S., & Heiden, E. (2012). Epidemiology of overuse and acute injuries among competitive collegiate athletes. *Journal of Athletic Training, 47*(2), 198–204.

Yiu, E., & Chan, R. (2003). Effect of hydration and vocal rest on the vocal fatigue in amateur karaoke singers. *Journal of Voice, 17,* 216–227.

4

JAZZ VOCAL CHARACTERISTICS

Now that you have learned some of the history of jazz as well as vocal technique, health, and wellness, we will learn about specific vocal jazz components. How do we know if a vocalist is a jazz singer? Is it the song or the singer that is jazz? With the mixture of styles and music of today, there can be confusion about who is really a jazz vocalist and who is not. The answer can be complex, but we do know there are certain recognizable characteristics that jazz vocalists and instrumentalists consistently exhibit. Yet how does one differentiate jazz vocals from other vocal styles? You might decide to go to a nightclub where a pop band is playing. The vocalist in the band is singing music by Adele and Lady Gaga. But you notice that during the set, she sings a jazz ballad, "My Funny Valentine" (music by Richard Rogers, lyrics by Lorenz Hart, 1937). The accompanying band is playing a funky groove behind the singer. The singer is singing the ballad in a funk groove, delivering the song in a pop rock style. If a pop vocalist sings "My Funny Valentine" with a pop-rock delivery, is she singing jazz?

Let's say that you want to be a jazz singer. You have not taken voice lessons before, so first you decide to take lessons focusing on the basics of vocal technique, which includes breath management. Over a six-month period, your voice teacher gives you scales, art songs, and arias to apply the techniques you are learning. Some of your friends may say, "Oh, you are studying opera," but in reality that may not be the case. You are being classically trained but not necessarily studying or singing opera. Just because a singer has had classical training does not mean that the singer has studied or trained in opera. Studying opera is more involved than one may think. Singers study for years to acquire the skill of singing opera repertoire, so singing songs from the classical repertoire does not mean you are proficient in opera. Yes, you have learned a few art songs and arias, but it does not mean your training will make you an opera singer. Anyone can sing familiar jazz standards, but not all who sing well-known jazz songs are jazz singers. Why?

To understand jazz, you need to develop hearing the intricacies of jazz. This includes phrasing, tone colors, chord progressions, rhythms, and improvisation. I call this your jazz ears! In the 1930s and the 1940s, jazz was the popular music of the time. The jazz singing style was very popular, and many aspiring vocalists wanted to emulate popular jazz singers they heard. Compared to the 1960s and 1970s and up to the present day, the 1940s record labels did not produce and record a large volume of music. During this time period, jazz recording artists received good exposure on the radio, which resulted in the sale of single records. And there were many opportunities for live performances—nightclubs, dances, concert halls, parties, and so on. As early as 1949, record companies began using rhythm and blues as a musical category instead of "race records."

American music began to change. Blues, rhythm and blues, and gospel recordings, primarily by Black artists, were more available to the public and received more radio exposure. As the style of popular music changed, young audiences emulated the pop, rock, and rhythm and blues music they heard. There was still jazz music, but by the 1960s in America, jazz was no longer the preeminent musical genre of the day. The electric guitar became more prominent in bands, and the music used a strong, heavy drumbeat instead of a swing groove. Vocalists began to sing more forcefully and loudly. Young audiences in the 1960s did not have the same level of exposure to jazz as the youth in the 1930s and 1940s did. By the 1960s, there were radios in automobiles, so not only could you listen to the radio at home, you could hear the popular hits of the day on the radio as you drove. More 45-rpm records were pressed, and more record players were prevalent in households. Jazz radio stations still existed, but there were more popular music radio stations playing the new popular music.

Communication in America became widespread via television, radio, and the telephone. This, along with more use of electric, amplified guitars, influenced the sound of the music as well as the style. So along with the most popular rock 'n' roll music being played on the radio, you could hear folk music, country music, rhythm and blues, gospel music, and Memphis soul. This variety of musical styles became part of the musical scene, from singer/songwriter Bob Dylan to rock and roll legend Elvis Presley, from country singer Merle Haggard to the Beatles. Some traditional jazz artists began to cross over into pop. Legendary jazz performers like Nat King Cole, Billy Eckstein, Dinah Washington, and Rosemary Clooney were coaxed by record producers to sing more popular music.

JAZZ TONAL QUALITY

The jazz singer's overall accepted tone quality changed through the years. What was first the conventional sound of the jazz voice, in the 1930s and 1940s, changed with the advent of electronic amplifiers and microphones. In the early days of jazz, singers whose delivery and approach utilized some jazz characteristics were considered jazz singers whether or not the tonal quality included vibrato. During the 1930s and 1940s, most jazz singers used their natural vibrato as part of singing. Voices could be full and heavy, like Sarah Vaughn's voice as she grew older, or more lilting, such as 1940s singers Doris Day, Ella Fitzgerald, Frank Sinatra, and Mel Tormé. When singer Joe Williams joined Count Basie's band in 1954, he gained a reputation as a strong blues singer. However, in his ballad singing, his voice had a beautiful full tone with a natural vibrato.

Listen to these two examples of Joe Williams listed below to hear the difference between his traditional blues singing and his ballad singing. By the 1940s, if not before, singers could be noted for a specific style and delivery even if in fact—as in the case of Joe Williams—the vocalist had other vocal attributes mostly unknown to the general public.

- W. York, "Everyday I Have the Blues," as recorded by Joe Williams with the Count Basie Orchestra, 2007
- R. Rogers and L. Hart, "You Are Too Beautiful" (1932), as recorded by Joe Williams, 2004 ♪

It should be noted that during this time period, even before most singers were considered jazz vocalists, anyone who could sing with expression and a good free tone was considered a good vocalist regardless of style. If a vocalist had a resonating voice with vibrato and good intonation, this was considered the norm.

As the 1950s approached, a more diverse group of singers became popular. This was coupled with the emergence of rock 'n' roll as America's popular music. At the same time, the bebop era emerged. This style of jazz utilized very fast tempos and showcased instrumentalists' solos. Some vocalists began to sing the solos of great jazz instrumentalists, while others added lyrics to an instrumental solo. A beautiful tone quality was not always used or necessary. Some vocalists used little vibrato in conjunction with the jazz style. For example, singer June Christy's voice did not have the round, full sound we associate with jazz singers of the time, but more of a straight tone with a little vibrato at the end of the phrase. Listen to June Christy's recording of "Something Cool" (B. Barnes, as recorded by June Christy, 1954).

LISTEN AND LEARN: BLUES AND JAZZ LEGENDS

Sister Rosetta Tharpe

In many ways, the style of pop singers mimicked the traditional blues singers, combined with gospel and rhythm and blues styles. However, this trend began prior to the 1960s. Sister Rosetta Tharpe was born in 1915. Rosetta's mother was a mandolin player and singer as well as a preacher. Encouraged by her mother, Rosetta played guitar and sang at an early age. Her training ground was singing and playing gospel music in church and in religious concerts with her mother. Eventually Sister Rosetta wrote her own songs. Infusing gospel music and blues into her singing of religious songs, she became popular in the South during the 1930s and 1940s. Sister Rosetta had a unique way of strumming her guitar that had a driving beat. Her style of singing combined gospel, spirituals, and traditional blues. In 1934, at age nineteen, Sister Rosetta recorded for Decca Records. Under the direction of jazzman John Hammond, she performed "Spirituals to Swing" at Carnegie Hall in 1938.

Although seldom recognized in present day, Sister Rosetta's guitar playing and singing style influenced many rock 'n' roll and soul artists including Aretha Franklin, Isaac Hayes, and Elvis Presley. When you listen to Sister Rosetta Tharpe play guitar and sing "Can't Sit Down," you will hear a strong blues delivery mixed with gospel. These elements in her vocal delivery and guitar accompaniment influenced many guitarists such as Chuck Berry and popular vocalists. Refer to Sister Rosetta singing in earlier recordings: "Down by the Riverside" (recorded by Sister Rosetta Tharpe in 1944, *Sister Rosetta Tharpe Complete Recorded Works 2, 1942–1944*, Document Records, 1996). ♪

Throughout the 1940s and 1950s, there were jazz artists like vocalist Dinah Washington who would later combine gospel and rhythm and blues. Dinah was noted as a jazz singer, but she was also strongly influenced by her gospel church music. Listen to singer Dinah Washington's two recordings listed below. These particular recordings exemplify the style of Dinah Washington incorporating a strong blues, gospel base into a jazz delivery: Dinah Washington singing "Evil Gal Blues" and later "Unforgettable." ♪

Mildred Bailey and Connie Boswell

Both Mildred Bailey and Connie Boswell were early jazz singers who combined the blues delivery with swing. Listening to these two influential early jazz vocalists will help you understand the evolution of jazz vocal style. Both singers, Mildred Bailey and Connie Boswell, were popular in the 1930s and 1940s, and both singers were very influenced by traditional blues singers.

Mildred Bailey sang with a sweet clear voice and good pitch. Her approach to phrasing was laid back, similar to Billie Holiday—in fact, the women were friends. In some of Mildred Bailey's recordings, you can detect a slightly fast vibrato toward the ends of some of her phrases as in "When It's Sleep Time Down South." Mildred Bailey was known as "Mrs. Swing" because she was able to phrase so well with the swing beat of the band. With her heartfelt delivery, she was able to incorporate a jazz swing groove into her interpretation. Mildred Bailey and her husband, vibraphonist Red Norvo, had a successful radio program so that her voice became well known to radio audiences. Some of her recordings like "Rockin Chair" became hits. Her natural swing feel and phrasing were a strong influence for other vocalists of the time. ♪

Connie Boswell and her sisters, Martha and Helvetia, were brought up in New Orleans. The sisters loved the hot jazz of New Orleans music. As young teenagers, the girls sang together in harmony. Martha played the piano accompaniment as she sang with her sisters. The sisters would sing off the back of a truck for a store opening or would be asked to sing together at yard parties. The sisters first recorded on a portable Victrola device in 1925. The trio later toured, settling in California and eventually in New York. The Boswell Sisters performed live, sang on live radio programs, and recorded on the Brunswick record label from 1931 to 1936. In addition to the trio work with her sisters, Connie also made records as a soloist. The recordings of Connie and her sisters demonstrate a unique combination of voices emulating horns and a strong bluesy delivery by Connie in her soloing.

Connie Boswell sang much like traditional blues singers, using subtle slides and blue notes. On some songs she would sing in more of a blues shout style for emphasis in a particular phrase. In swing tunes, in slow or fast tempos, Connie Boswell possessed an innate sense of timing. You can hear Connie's strong blues affect on her solo work in "Heebie Jeebies." A young Ella Fitzgerald heard the Boswells on the radio and also played one of their popular songs on a record player at home. Ella listened to Connie's solo in the song "The Object of My Affection" and has often stated that she was her primary influence.

Billie Holiday

To further understand traditional jazz vocal characteristics, let's compare two great jazz artists in regard to jazz characteristics and style—Billie Holiday and Ella Fitzgerald.

Figure 4.1.   Billie Holiday. *Library of Congress/Gottlieb Collection*

As a young girl, Billie Holiday heard recordings of Louis Armstrong, Bessie Smith, and Mamie Smith. When Billie began to sing professionally in the 1930s, she borrowed her phrasing mostly from Louis Armstrong's voice and trumpet playing. In a conversational delivery, Billie would elongate some of the phrases within a song, much like Armstrong's trumpet. In the early years, we can hear a somewhat clearer tone and flexibility in Billie's voice, but often Billie did not showcase the tone of her voice. Instead, her focus was her expression and phrasing. In most instances, Billie Holiday would approach her singing of jazz songs in a speak/sing way with little or no vibrato. On the last word of a phrase, Billie would use more vocal tone and add vibrato.

Listen to Billie Holiday's "Your Mother's Son-in Law" from the 1933 recording with Benny Goodman and his Orchestra. In line with the style of the early 1930s, the band played in a fast swing groove reminiscent of King Oliver's Jazz Band, legends of the New Orleans scene. Goodman's band starts off the song, playing a full chorus before the vocalist comes in. Billie's solo vocals sound much like traditional blues singer but without any typical blues slides or blue notes. Two years later in "What a Little Moonlight Will Do," the band first plays a fast swing with a two-beat feel. Billie enters the song with a relaxed laid-back rhythm over the fast two-beat feel. Essentially, she is singing outside of the song's originally written rhythm. This method became part of Billie Holiday's style that set her apart from other early jazz vocalists.

Listening to Billie Holiday's mid- to late 1930s recordings, you can hear her finesse and development of rhythmic phrasing. Even though Billie Holiday's voice became ragged as years went by, her phrasing was impeccable. An example of Billie Holiday's phrasing is this particular version of "I Cover the Waterfront" with the Eddy Heywood Orchestra. When you listen to this recording, pay close attention to how Billie Holiday phrases. You will notice that she back phrases or lays behind the beat. Billie Holiday tended not to follow the written rhythm of most songs. See figure 4.2 for a few measures of the original notation of the jazz standard "I'll Be Seeing You." ♪

See figure 4.3 for Billie Holiday's version of same excerpt.

Billie Holiday exemplified jazz rhythmic phrasing in her performances and her recordings. By her last recordings in the late 1950s, her voice was weak and she sang with less range. Her tonal quality sounded raspy and often mournful, yet her unique approach to phrasing was still present.

A few suggested recordings from Billie Holiday's later recordings you should listen to include "I Cried for You," "I'm a Fool to Want You," and "I'll Never Smile Again." ♪

Ella Fitzgerald

In 1937, at the age of eighteen, Ella began singing with the Chick Webb Band. Influenced by listening to singer Connie Boswell, Ella tried to sing

Figure 4.2. Original Four Bars of "I'll Be Seeing You." *Irving Kahal/Sammy Fain*

like her idol. Her light and lyrical sound was agile with a three-octave range. Although Ella's lyrical voice and Connie Boswell's alto-timbred voice were not alike in sound, it is important to note Boswell's influence upon Ella's recordings. In Ella's 1935 recording of "Love and Kisses," you can hear the influence within Ella's phrasing. Ella approaches the

I'LL BE SEEING YOU
As recorded by Billie Holiday, 1944, Commodore Records

Transcr. by D. Schachter

Figure. 4.3 Billie Holiday's Interpretation of Four Bars of "I'll Be Seeing You." *Daniela Schachter*

melody first by singing a grace note a step above the melody and then slides downward into the note. Connie Boswell does this frequently in her recordings both as a soloist and in the Boswell Sisters vocal arrangements. Ella internalizes the swing groove and phrases in a relaxed manner. These two elements go together in regard to singing jazz. ♪

Two examples of Connie Boswell's solo work singing with her sisters, the Boswell Sisters, are on the songs "I Thank You Mr. Moon" and "Minnie the Moocher's Wedding Day." Early examples of young Ella Fitzgerald's singing are "A Little Bit Later On" and the song "Jumpin' Jive," from Ella Fitzgerald's recording with orchestra, live at the Savoy Ballroom, New York City, in 1939. ♪

During the 1940s big band era, Ella's singing continued to develop. In the early to mid-1940s, the band was more the feature than the singer. Big bands would play a chorus or two of a song, then the vocalist sang one chorus, and the band would continue to play after the vocals. During the second chorus of a song, band members might play an improvised solo. Generally speaking, the vocalist would sit off to the side until it was time to sing. Ella Fitzgerald sat on a chair next to the band, listening to the horn players soloing while waiting her turn to sing. As time went on, Ella incorporated the horn riffs and solos of the band into her own singing, imitating the horn players' phrasing.

Figure 4.4.   Ella Fitzgerald. *Library of Congress/Gottlieb Collection*

As Ella's voice matured, she maintained the light timbre in her upper range but also developed and utilized her lower range. Throughout her singing career, Ella was known for her vocal flexibility. She would utilize all of her vocal range in her solos and could improvise to very fast tempos. Fitzgerald's outstanding improvised scat singing is still considered to be beyond compare and remains the model and ideal for jazz singers past and present. Ella Fitzgerald's musical ear was remarkable. She sang expressively with a clear vocal tone, sang the given lyrics of a song, and then added her own improvised interpretation through what is known as scat singing.

Ella often sang the song "Oh, Lady Be Good" in her many live performances. In fact, there are several recorded versions of Ella singing this song. You can listen to all the versions, but make sure you listen to the version of "Oh, Lady Be Good" recorded in 1957 (note this particular version is timed at four minutes and three seconds, but on some remastered CDs, the time is listed as four minutes and four seconds). ♪

See figure 4.5 for the original melody and rhythm of "Oh, Lady Be Good."

Figure 4.5. Original Melody of "Oh, Lady Be Good." *Music and Lyrics by George Gershwin and Ira Gershwin ©1924 (Renewed) WB Music Corp. All Rights Reserved.*

Oh. Lady Be Good (Ella Fitzgerald Scat)

Recorded January 7, 1959 in Los Angeles
From "The Essential Ella Fitzgerald: The Great Songs", Verve 517170

Transcribed by Justin Binek

Figure 4.6. Ella Fitzgerald's Interpretation of "Oh, Lady Be Good." *Sound Music Publications*

See figure 4.6 for a short transcription of Ella's version of "Oh, Lady Be Good" from Los Angeles, 1957.

Listen to the same song again recorded ten years before in 1947. In the 1947 version, Ella scats effortlessly through a chorus, emulates a horn riff during the second chorus, and then inserts words to the song "A Tisket A Tasket." She also sings a section of her improvisation imitating a tenor or baritone saxophone replying back to herself in more of a trumpet sound. Ten years later, in the 1957 version, Ella further developed her improvisation to entail not only scat but also improvised lyrics. ♪

Ella Fitzgerald possessed great vocal flexibility and agility, singing fast passages with or without words with ease. But if you listen to her ballad singing, you will note her feeling and sincere delivery. She phrases in such a way as to make us feel the words of the song by holding on to a word for emphasis, slightly leaning on a note or accenting it as in a conversation.

Billie Holiday and Ella Fitzgerald both naturally used conversational phrasing, relaxed and laid-back phrasing, vocal inflections, subtle use of accents on a word/note, and improvised rhythmic phrasing. Billie Holiday excelled in rhythmic phrasing and her subtle use of inflections for emphasis. Ella's improvisation was not only rhythmic but also melodic—varying the melody particularly after the first chorus of a song. She also set the bar for wordless, improvised vocals. Like Billie Holiday, Ella had an excellent sense of timing, using her wide vocal range within her melodic improvisation. Great jazz artists like Billie Holiday and Ella Fitzgerald still influence many vocalists of today. As aspiring jazz singers, it's important to learn from the great jazz singers by borrowing their phrasing while discovering your own vocal sound.

JAZZ SINGERS AND BEBOP

The bebop era showcased instrumental virtuosity at fast tempos and further improvisation. Instead of an instrumentalist taking one solo within the framework of a jazz standard, he or she might take two or even three. Some jazz vocalists embraced the era of bebop while others remained steeped in traditional jazz. Singing instrumental solos was and is a unique skill. The actual solo lines might be easy for a saxophone or trumpet to play at a fast tempo. However, vocal improvisation not only requires vocalists to hear harmony and chordal structure to accurately create and emulate hornlike melodic lines, it also requires overall vocal control and flexibility of one's voice.

Fast tempos are often even more difficult for the singer in regard to pitch and note accuracy. The singers have no buttons to push or strings to pluck. Instead, we only have our ears and voices. There are many live and recorded examples of instrumentalists and vocalists improvising and trading musical ideas with each other simultaneously. If you listen to Ella Fitzgerald's version of Duke Ellington's composition "Cottontail" recorded in 1956, you will hear Ella's call and response with the saxophone player after the instrumental solos, which showcases a particularly stunning example of vocal improvisation.

Anita O'Day cut her jazz teeth during the big band era. Even during the late 1930s and 1940s, Anita individualized her style by wearing a suit jacket with a skirt instead of the usual evening gown. She was bold in her individuality and in her singing. O'Day sang the usual big band repertoire, but by the 1950s she branched out to more difficult instrumental songs as heard in her recording of "Four Brothers." Anita O'Day's approach to improvisation was very hornlike and she could scat at a fast tempo. Her rhythm and musical instinct was far ahead of the usual big band swing singers. Anita crossed over musical boundaries and is included as one of the vocalists that led the way to bebop. To hear Anita's sense of timing listen to "Sweet Georgia Brown" (B. Bernie, M. Pickard, and K. Casey [1925], as recorded by Anita O'Day, 1958) and her unique version of "Tea for Two" (V. Youmans and I. Caesar [1925] as recorded by Anita O'Day, 1958). ♪

Jazz singer Betty Carter began singing with the Lionel Hampton band at age sixteen in 1948. The story goes that before joining the Hampton band, Betty was sitting in with the notable jazz saxophonist Charlie Parker when he played in her hometown of Detroit. She also had the opportunity to perform with the influential bebop trumpeter Dizzy Gillespie. Betty Carter's talent and jazz aspirations were in the bebop style. Samplings of Better Carter's early work and later in her career include the songs "Frenesi," recorded in 1956, and "My Favorite Things," recorded in 1980. ♪

Some of the instrumental solos attracted singers like Eddie Jefferson. Starting out as a dancer, Jefferson began writing lyrics. Sometime in 1949, Eddie Jefferson heard saxophonist Charlie Parker. He began writing lyrics to Parker's solos as well as lyrics from other instrumentalist's solo works. This was not an easy task since many of these solos were at fast tempos! In 1948 Charlie Parker recorded "Parker's Mood" on Savoy Records. Jefferson eventually recorded this song with his lyrics during 1949–1950. One of the most popular lyrics that Jefferson wrote was based on the song "I'm in the Mood for Love" (McHugh/Fields). Eddie Jefferson called it "Moody's Mood for Love," writing lyrics to saxophonist James Moody's sax solo. Although Jefferson was not the first to record "Moody's Mood for Love," he became recognized for his writing of lyrics to solos until his death in 1979. Certainly there were others who wrote lyrics to instrumental solos. However, Eddie Jefferson was one of the most prominent lyricists of jazz vocalese during the 1940s through 1960s. ♪

Listen to both King Pleasure's recordings of "Moody's Mood for Love," 1954. Jefferson's collections of songs can be found on remastered CD issues.

Figure 4.7. Transcription of James Moody's Solo in "I'm in the Mood For Love." *Words and Music by James Moody, Dorothy Fields, and Jimmy McHugh ©1935 (Renewed) EMI Robbins Catalog (Publishing) and Alfred Music (Print). All Rights Reserved.*

THE STORYTELLERS

In chapter 1, we briefly discussed blues singers who were strong story-tellers. Some jazz singers are masters at telling a story through the lyrics of a ballad. Unlike most pop singers, jazz vocalists can choose to sing a verse or a portion of a song or an introduction not in any set tempo. The singer creates and sings improvised rhythmic phrases. Jazz singers and instrumentalists use the musical term *rubato*, sometimes referred to as ad-lib, with no set time feel as an introduction into a song. In other words, the tempo can fluctuate per phrase. This freedom, with no particular rhythmic time limit, allows the jazz vocalist to improvise a song or song verse out of tempo. As if delivering a poem, the singer can pause between phrases, hold out a note for emphasis, and then decide to sing a phrase at a faster pace—all as part of the song interpretation. This interpretive skill is a way of introducing a song, often delivered in a subtle or intimate way that tends to draw in the listener. A singer can hold onto a word or bend a note for emphasis and also use subtle or gradual dynamics.

Learning to sing a verse rubato may seem easy, but not all jazz vocalists are masters of this technique. The vocalist and accompanying instrument, a pianist or guitarist, have to be musically coordinated. The instrumentalist accompanying the singer listens to the singer's phrasing and plays supportive lines behind the singer. Sometimes the accompanist leads the singer into the next phrase; other times the vocalist leads the accompanist.

Nancy Wilson is a singer that began her career in the blues and jazz realm but also crossed over into other musical genres later in her career. Her 1960 recording of "Guess Who I Saw Today" is an example of a rubato introduction to a song. With certain singers and songs, a rubato introduction or ending of a song can be a very effective way to tell the story. When listening to singer Nancy Wilson's vocal delivery of "Guess Who I Saw Today," we immediately note her gift for storytelling. Her conversational phrasing with pauses, slides into a word, emphasis on a word, and use of dynamics demonstrates an improvisational phrasing skill that delivers the song in a unique and intimate way. It is difficult to visually show Nancy Wilson's phrasing in notation. Here is an excerpt from the original "Guess Who I Saw Today:" ♪

GUESS WHO I SAW TODAY

Words and Music by MURRAY GRAND
and ELISSE BOYD

Figure 4.8. Original Melody of "Guess Who I Saw Today." *Words and Music by Murray Grand and Elisse Boyd ©1952 (Renewed) Sony/ATV Music Publishing LLC. All Rights Administered by Sony/ATV Music Publishing LLC, 424 Church Street Suite 1200, Nashville, TN 37219. International Copyright Secured. All Rights Reserved. Reprinted with Permission of Hal Leonard Corporation.*

Here is Nancy Wilson's version:

Figure 4.9. Nancy Wilson's Interpretation of "Guess Who I Saw Today."
D. Schachter

Compare Nancy Wilson's recording of "Guess Who I Saw Today" with her 1961 recordings with saxophonist Cannonball Adderly. Jazz vocalist Carmen McRae also crafted this delivery. Listen to Carmen's recording of "Dindi" as an example. Included in the group of expert storytellers are Blossom Dearie, Frank Sinatra, Nat King Cole, Shirley Horn, and Abbey Lincoln.

COMPARING JAZZ TO OTHER STYLES

Vocalist John Legend is considered an R&B/pop vocalist. He sings the song "Stay with You" (S. J. Anderson, J. Stephen, F. Gillies, and A. Skylark, *Get Lifted*, Sony, 2004 [Track 9]) in a soulful way. His phrases (the lyrical lines) are short; he does not hold out notes in the verse. The accompaniment is played in a pop groove or rhythm. As you listen, you will hear John Legend embellish notes on the syllable "oh." He uses his falsetto voice within the song—that is, the very high range of the male voice. Frank Sinatra's phrasing and singing of the lyrics are quite different. His phrasing is more conversational, like someone talking to another. The groove of the song has an underlying swing feel. Sinatra sometimes holds out the notes. The style is relaxed. Sinatra does not use falsetto. When a jazz singer such as Sinatra holds a word over the bar line, or drags out a word within the phrase, that is a part of his or her unique interpretation, but it also is part of jazz improvisation. The notation written by the composer is rhythmically and often melodically altered. Pop vocals are different. The vocal delivery is usually more abrupt. Pop singers do improvise, but they approach it differently. Rather than altering the rhythm or singing over the bar line, pop and R&B vocalists may approach a phrase or a word by singing a series of notes to a single syllable or word—this is called a melisma. The singers' performances are also distinguished by the instrumentation they use. A typical jazz vocal combo would include a basic rhythm section consisting of piano, upright bass, and drums, and occasionally guitar. In the song "If I Had You" (J. Campbell, R. Connelly, and T. Shapiro [1928], as recorded by Frank Sinatra, *The Columbia Years 1942–1953: The Complete Recordings Vol. 6*, Sony Music, 1993 [Track 21]), Sinatra performs with a similar rhythm section setup but adds a small string section, as well as a flutist. The instrumentation of John Legend's recording is heavy on the beat, and the recording uses a drum set as well as a MIDI percussion track. ♪

James Taylor "Her Town Too" and Kelley Hunt "Brick By Brick"

"Her Town Too" (J. D. Souther, J. Taylor, and W. Wachtel, 1981 [Track 2]) is a pop ballad—the beat of the song has an eighth-note feel. The instrumentation includes electric keyboard, guitar, electric bass, drums, and backing vocalist. James Taylor sings in a relaxed conversational way, but his phrasing does not contain melodic or rhythmic improvisation in the same way that a jazz singer's would. Taylor is considered a folk/pop vocalist. ♪

Kelley Hunt is a blues vocalist and pianist. She accompanies herself in this original tune, with her band on electric bass, guitar, and drums. The band is playing an eighth-note rock beat with a blues groove. Hunt's vocals are reminiscent of the traditional blues singers with a bit of gospel style added—she uses blues-type embellishments in her delivery. Although Kelley's vocal delivery is blues-based, her delivery is not like Ella Fitzgerald or Billie Holiday. She sings more in a forceful way, with shorter phrases ending with a "blues lick." At times, her delivery has more of an edge, rather than the softer melodic sound of Ella Fitzgerald or the rhythmic phrasing of Billie Holiday. Listen to blues singer Kelley Hunt on her composition "Brick by Brick" (K. Hunt, 2000 [Track 2]). ♪

All the characteristics of the blues style can be applied to jazz vocals. However, the main element that varies in singing jazz is the overall vocal delivery and approach. Jazz music and chord progressions are generally more complex. Jazz chord progressions were unlike classical or written sheet music. The structure of jazz chords includes dissonance. So the chord structure would contain a triad but could also contain a seventh, ninth, flat fifth and so on. Because the chordal structure added extensions of the chord (sevenths, ninths, elevens, thirteens), jazz instrumentalists and singers were able to expand their improvisation based on the jazz chordal structure. Jazz band members would improvise one or two choruses of a song. The jazz vocalist might improvise by scat singing a chorus or by singing the lyric while improvising the melody. Sometimes a horn player and the singer would trade off every four measures answering each other's improvised solo.

JAZZ FUSION

Fusion is defined as a mixture or a combination of things. Jazz fusion in today's musical world is everywhere. In the 1960s it could be the fusion between jazz and rock. So, for example, the arrangement of the jazz standard such as "My Funny Valentine" would be played with jazz chords. But the rhythm section would likely be composed of electric bass. The drummer would use sticks and the rhythm would not swing. Rock groups that fused jazz together with a different groove include Blood Sweat and Tears and the group Chicago. In general, the rock element is stronger than the jazz in jazz fusion. Jazz trumpeter Miles Davis experimented with jazz fusion in the 1960s. By the 1980s, jazz and R&B and funk became part of the term jazz fusion. Even the great jazz artist Sarah Vaughn ventured into the pop world, recording a song called "Broken Hearted Melody" (S. Edwards and H. David [1958]) in the 1950s. The song became a hit and made younger audiences aware of Sarah Vaughn. But she was criticized by jazz purists for selling out jazz to popular music.

Jazz fusion combines jazz with other styles: jazz and R&B, jazz and Latin, and jazz and rock. The instrumentalists and the vocalists have jazz as a basis but combine another style, fusing them together. In nearly all cases, fusion singers have had experience in both singing and listening to jazz. Singers who are known for this artistry include Al Jarreau, Ledisi, Diane Reeves, Bobbie McFerrin, Rachelle Farrell, Cassandra Wilson, and Tania Maria. When you listen to these singers, you will hear the jazz influence in regard to phrasing and improvisation. Yet, at the same time, you may hear rhythm and blues licks, songs with pop lyrics, different musical arrangements, tempos, and groove. It is interesting to also note that many of the instrumentalists that back up fusion vocalists are jazz players.

Even in the pop and rock world, many of the instrumental musicians have blues and jazz as their roots. By knowing and experiencing traditional jazz vocal style, a vocalist can develop strong improvisational and musical skills that can serve as a stepping-stone to other styles of today. Listen to the following suggested recordings as an example of jazz fusion.

- Al Jarreau, "Boogie Down" (M. Omartian and A. Jarreau [1983, Track 2]),
- Diane Reeves, "Better Days" (T. D. Lorrich and D. Reeves [1987]),
- Chaka Khan (*Echoes of an Era* [1982]),
- Lou Rawls, "You'll Never Find Another Love Like Mine" (K. Gamble and L. Huff [1976]), and
- Gregory Porter, "I Fall in Love Too Easily" (J. Styne and S. Cahn [1954], *Liquid Spirit*, 2013). ♪

A jazz singer is so adept at his or her skill that a person new to jazz can find it difficult to detect just what makes a particular singer "jazz." Often we hear a vocalist singing a traditional jazz standard. We listen indirectly to the instrumentation, the tempo, and groove. When we listen to a singer with a band, we listen to the singers' tone, lyrics, and meaning of the song. What are more difficult to hear are the subtle differences in vocal delivery and phrasing. To be fair, today's singers are not generally exposed to the history of American blues and jazz beginnings, including the interaction between the jazz instrumentalists and vocalist.

In-depth jazz vocal characteristics require strong jazz ears, listening to the groove of the band and the chord progressions, and listening to the approach and delivery of the solo instrument, including the vocalist. In most instances a jazz vocalist singing traditional jazz repertoire maintains a free-sounding tone that is not forced or strained. Phrases are held out, and some words are held over the bar line. The jazz singer internalizes the overall swing groove of the rhythm section while improvising the phrases rhythmically. In review, jazz vocal characteristics include:

- free-sounding tone,
- laid-back, relaxed phrasing,
- holding a note/word over the bar line,

- improvised rhythmic phrasing,
- melodic improvisation,
- use of subtle vocal inflections and dynamics,
- conversational delivery, and
- varying the tempo.

In the upcoming chapters, you will learn how to listen to jazz music and how to develop your jazz ears.

BIBLIOGRAPHY

Arlen, H., Koehler, T., & Calloway, C. (1931). Minnie the moocher's wedding day. *The Boswell Sisters—That's How Rhythm Was Born* [CD]. Columbia/ Legacy Art Deco. (1995).

Arnheim, G., Freed, A., & Lyman, A. (1923). I cried for you. *Billie Holiday, Lady in Autumn: The Best of the Verve Years* [CD]. Polygram Records. (1991).

Atkins, B. (1926). Heebie jeebies. *Boswell Sisters: Darktown Strutters Ball* [CD]. Classic Records. (2008).

Baer, A. (1931). I thank you mister moon. *The Boswell Sisters Brunswick, Vol.1* [CD]. Collectibles. (2000).

Feather, L., & Hampton, L. (1944). Evil gal blues. (Recorded by Dinah Washington). *Dinah Washington's Greatest Hits 1946–53* [CD]. Acrobat Music. (2005).

Friml, R., Stoll, G., & Webster, P. F. (1935). Love and kisses. (Recorded by Ella Fitzgerald). *Ella Fitzgerald: The Early Years Part I* [CD]. GRP/Decca. (1997).

Gershwin, G., & Gershwin, I. (1921). Oh, lady be good. *Ella Fitzgerald At the Opera House* [CD]. Polygram Records. (1990).

Gordan, I. (1951). Unforgettable. *Dinah Washington Unforgettable* [CD]. Mercury. (1991).

Heyman, E., & Green, J. 1933. I cover the waterfront. (Recorded by Billie Holiday). Commodore. 1944.

Livingston, J., & Neiburg, A. J. (1930). A little bit later on. (Recorded by Ella Fitzgerald). *Ella Fitzgerald: The Early Years Part 1* [CD]. GRP Records. (1995).

Lowe, R. (1939). I'll never smile again. *Billie Holiday: Last Recording* [CD]. Polygram Records. (1990).

Rene, L., Rene, O., & Muse, C. (1931). When it's sleep time down south. *Mildred Bailey Vol.1: Sweet Beginnings* [CD]. Old Masters. (1995).

Rodgers, R., & Hammerstein II, O. (1991). My favorite things. *The Audience with Betty Carter* [CD]. Verve. (Bet-Car Records 1980).

Wolf, J., Herron, J., & Sinatra, Frank. (1951) I'm a fool to want you. *Lady in Satin. Billie Holiday* [CD]. Sony. (1997).

Woods, H. (1934). What a little moonlight can do. *The Essential Billie Holiday: The Columbia Years* [CD]. Sony Legacy. (2010).

Various. (2007). Oh, lady be good. *Lullabies of Birdland Ella Fitzgerald* [CD]. Verve/Decca. (1947).

Various. (1996). Frenesi. *Meet Betty Carter & Ray Bryant* [CD]. Sony. (Columbia 1956).

5

DEVELOPING JAZZ EARS

HOW TO LISTEN TO JAZZ

Listening to music casually is easy. We naturally snap our fingers, tap our feet, and move our body to the rhythm. We hum along with the melody or sing the lyrics to a particular song we like. Cultivating a critical musical ear for the intricacies of jazz, however, is more of a challenge!

Listen to What?

In general, beginning singers are not accustomed to listening to the specific notes being played on the bass or hearing jazz chord progressions. Most often sheet music for arias, music theater, and pop songs include piano accompaniment with the melody being mirrored in the right hand of the pianist. Most of us are used to hearing the melody first and foremost. In contrast, jazz standard lead sheets do not include specific chord voicings or written-out notes within the chord. Instead, the lead sheet shows the melody (the "head") written out with chord symbols above the staff. The role of a jazz pianist changes when he or she is accompanying a jazz vocalist. When accompanying a singer, the pianist does not play the melody, only the chord progressions. For example, choose a jazz standard song by a jazz artist such as Ella Fitzgerald, Sarah Vaughan, Mel Tormé, or Joe Williams, or try listening to Chet Baker's trumpet playing on a recording. Listen to the bass line instead of the singer or horn player. Choose a recording with piano, bass, and drums and possibly horn players as well. The song could be a slow or medium swing tempo or a ballad. Next, try to sing the rhythm of the bass line and some of the notes once you've learned some of the basic rhythm.

Next, using the same recording, listen closely to the drummer. Try to emulate the drum beat rhythm. Use your foot or hands or both to create the same sort of drum groove you hear. While you are tapping out the rhythmic groove with your feet and hands, sing the melody with the singer. Also, try going back to the bass line or the bass rhythmic pattern. The bass and drums provide a pulse that lays down the overall tempo and swing groove. This is what helps us feel the swing.

When we hear a song we know, we are accustomed to feeling the beat and rhythm of the song. When we hear and feel the beat, our ears tend to go right to the melody and then to the words of the song that fit with the groove. We hear the harmony played by the piano or guitarist in a general way as the chord progressions go by supporting the melody. Most of us can tell if something a pianist or guitarist is playing does not sound right. However, since jazz chords are often complex, it can be difficult to hear exactly what the pianist or guitarist is actually playing. In jazz, the chords can be inverted from root position, to first, second, or third position, as well as have added tensions or extensions to the chords. Any instrument that you can use to play chords—piano, organ, or guitar—allows for the position of the chords to be changed (inverted) rather than always played in a set position.

Different chord voicings change the way we hear a chord, and the melody may be hard to hear within the chord. If you are an inexperienced jazz vocalist singing with a jazz pianist, it is easy for you to miss your cue into the song if you are not accustomed to hearing different jazz chord voicings.

Today, thanks to the Internet, you can actually hear how different jazz piano voicings sound. You can find examples on websites such as YouTube and www.freejazzlessons.com.

CHORD SCALE EXERCISES

SHAPIRO

Figure 5.1. Jazz Chord Inversions ♪

Listening to Instrumental Solos

Have you ever attended a jazz concert or nightclub where a saxophone player takes a solo? The saxophonist solos through the form of the song once and often decides to take another solo starting at the beginning. Sometimes a horn player solos through more than two choruses. It's easy to become lost as to where or what she or he is playing. Suddenly the melody of a familiar jazz standard is so obscured that it becomes difficult to discern where the soloist is within the song. This can also happen when listening to a vocalist sing two choruses of a standard jazz song in scat!

In the jazz idiom, an improvised solo is based on the same chord progressions of a standard jazz song. Listening to jazz instrumentalists can help us understand more about improvisation and help you with your own vocal improvisation. When we listen to trumpeter and singer Chet Baker's solos—both on trumpet and sung—we can try to catch some of the improvisational ways he phrases and solos.

Choose a familiar jazz standard you know and try singing the melody without the words. When you hear the trumpet solo at the beginning of song, hum or sing the melody at the same time—while the trumpet player is playing. This will help you understand the melodic variation of the improviser while at the same time understanding where you and the soloist are in the song. Examples include Chet Baker in "But Not for Me" and "All the Things You Are."

Sax player Charlie Parker was one of the leaders of the bebop era. Parker's long solos became songs within a song. For example, Parker's composition "Ornithology" has the same chord changes as the standard "How High the Moon." Basically Parker's "Ornithology" was a different melody put to an existing song. Listen to Charlie Parker play "Anthropology" and "Ornithology." Then listen to recordings of jazz singers who sing Charlie Parker's solos. Some examples are vocalists Sheila Jordan singing "Bird Alone" and "Confirmation" and also Kitty Margolis singing "Anthropology." ♪

The Rhythm Section

You may wonder why, as a singer, it is important for you to listen to the bass and drums in recorded examples or live performances. A jazz singer's phrasing depends upon the rhythm section's groove or time. Even though the pianist is playing complementary chords as you sing, if the bass and drummer are not together, as a whole, the song you are singing won't sound together with the band. The rhythm section and the horn players set the stage for vocal improvisation. As jazz singers, our musical ideas of phrasing and improvisation should work with the music the band is playing.

The improvisational and song structure format within a trio is not always set. For aspiring jazz singers, learning to hear jazz chord progressions is an important part of cultivating your jazz ears. Remember to listen to the bass and drums and then listen to the piano or guitar chords. Generally in a jazz trio (piano, bass, and drums), the pianist will play the melody of the song through. The pianist or guitarists can add melodic alterations but will generally still touch upon the original melody. After one chorus of the song is played, there is an instrumental solo, or the pianist will solo through the song twice. The pianist then returns back to the melody at the beginning of the song and plays once more through until the end of the song.

During a jazz set, the singer usually sings one full chorus of a song. Then the pianist takes a solo through the form of the song. The whole rhythm section can decide to take individual solos on a specific song—or not. The bassist may take a few solos and/or the drummer may take a solo. Sometimes the bassist and drummer trade fours. This means that through the form of the song or the complete song, the bassist may solo for four measures and then in response to the bassist, the drummer solos for four measures and so on until the end of the song. Trading fours with the bassist and the drums can also include the pianist. For example, the pianist can solo on the first sixteen measures of a jazz standard song, the bassist can solo over the next B section or bridge, and the drummer can solo over the last half of the song. Then the singer comes back in at the beginning of the song, or it can also be the last half of the song. There are several combinations of instrumental soloing including each instrument soloing over the complete song.

The jazz singer has to hear and know when to come back into a song after the instrumental solos. How can you tell when to come in after all the instrumental solos? How do you hear your starting note back into the song? Once you know the melody of the song, you can simply count the measures of the song silently while the instrumentalists solo. This works for most jazz standards that have a sixteen-measure verse, eight measures of the B or bridge section, and eight measures of the last verse. You can silently hum the melody to yourself as you hear each instrumentalist solo through the form of the song. In addition to doing this in a rehearsal or singing with a trio in a club, listen to recordings of a vocalist with a jazz trio and then try to count measures on the solos. Then try humming the melody while the soloist is playing. After a while, you will know where you are in the song even when an instrumentalist is soloing. The goal is to know the song and chord progressions so well that you no longer have to count measures and instead listen to the instrumentalist solo. Listening to the solo can give you ideas regarding your own improvised solo. In some cases when the instrumentalist solos, the singer may trade fours, vocally echoing some of the instrumentalist's musical ideas.

The Bassist

What is the bass playing? The string bass in jazz provides part of the groove. It gives the song depth in relationship to the jazz chord progressions, beat, and tempo. Bassists help keep the song together along with the drummer. Together the bassist and the drummer create the time feel of the song. In a swing tempo, the bassist can walk the bass. This means that the bass player outlines the chord one note per beat, hitting every beat per measure.

To really hear what the bass is playing, it's best to listen with good stereo speakers. If you use an iPod, your computer, or any mp3 player, listen through good headphones so you can hear the definition of the bass sound. Try to adjust the sound so that the bass is boosted. It is essential as a jazz singer that you hear the articulation of the bass rather than just hearing a low or dark, boomy sound. Listen to the bass on these suggested recordings:

- "Willow Weep For Me" with Oscar Pettiford on bass,
- "Fascinating Rhythm" with Milt Hinton on bass,
- "There is No Greater Love" with Paul Chambers on bass,
- "In a Mellow Tone" with Ron Carter on bass, Helen Merrill, voice,
- "I Thought About You" with Ray Brown on bass, Diana Krall, voice, and
- "Speak Love" with Ray Brown on bass, Monty Alexander on piano. ♪

The Drummer and the Groove

The initial role of the drummer is to maintain the tempo. However, the bass player also must keep the time. The bass player and the drummer work together to lock in the tempo. In other words, the bass player and the drummer have to synchronize musically. The ride cymbal is the drummer's swing. In basic terms, a swing feel occurs when the bass player plays a string at the same time as the ride cymbal. The best way to detect this is to listen to recorded examples of trios, piano or guitar, bass, and drums. In order for there to be a steady tempo and groove, the bass player and drummer have to listen to each other and play as a unit. Listen to bassist Ray Brown and drummer Gerryck King on "Easy Does It" and Jeff Hamilton on drums on "Kelly's Blues." In jazz terms, they provide great examples of locking in the groove. ♪

The Pianist

The pianist has more than one function. With a trio, the pianist comps the chord progressions, generally avoiding the root of the chord since the bassist is playing the root note. In an instrumental trio setting (piano, bass, and drums), the pianist generally plays the melody in the right hand while playing the chord in the left hand. When the bassist takes a solo, the pianist can decide to play an accompanying chord on some of the downbeats per measure or lay out completely over the bass line. While the bass player and drummer are maintaining the beat, the pianist can solo over the song, improvising melodically and rhythmically.

When a singer is part of the trio, the function of the pianist changes. The pianist voices the chord progressions to complement the melody sung by the vocalist. The bass and the drums keep the tempo and groove. The pianist follows the vocalist's phrasing, complementing the singer with the chord voicings and progression he or she plays. For listening practice, listen to the following recordings:

- *Intimate Ella,*
- *Ella with the Tommy Flanagan Trio,*
- *George Shearing Quintet with Nancy Wilson,* and
- *Sarah Vaughan Live at Mister Kelly's.*

Also listen to the young jazz artist mentored by Jon Hendricks and bassist John Clayton, Sachal Vasandani on "Travelin' Light."

The Horn Players

Since the early days of jazz, musicians on saxophone, trumpet, and trombone have always been part of jazz. During the big band era of the

1940s, vocalists sang with a large big band consisting of one voice with five saxophones (two alto, two tenor, and one baritone sax), four trombones, and four or five trumpets. Imagine what it would be like to sing with such a big band wailing behind you!

In later years and at present, a jazz singer typically works with a rhythm section with an added horn or horns. There are instances where a vocalist may work only with a pianist or guitarist. For our discussion in this chapter, we will talk about the vocalist with a rhythm section and one horn player—a saxophone or trumpet player.

When the horn player is in a band with the vocalist, he or she has two functions. In the band, the horn player is soloist and also a complement to the solo vocals. Before you go further, listen to distinctive jazz saxophonists such as Johnny Hodges and Charlie Parker and trumpet players Louis Armstrong, Chet Baker, Miles Davis, and Dizzy Gillespie. The aforementioned artists are only a starting point—there are many, many great jazz horn players!

The Instrumental Soloist

The best soloists are musicians that know jazz standards well. This means they know the melody and the form of the song (verse, chorus, or bridge). This also includes knowing the chord progressions that work within the song.

Typically, in a jazz performance, the singer will sing through one chorus of a song. Let's say the song is a ballad, for example: "Crazy He Calls Me" (B. Russell and C. Segman [1949]). You have just sung through the song. Now the pianist begins at the top of the song. The trumpet player begins the solo. The trumpet player sings by playing his or her instrument, improvising a countermelody that blends well with the song's chord progression. Listen to the horn player's phrasing. Within the solo, the trumpet player may speed up some of the notes within a phrase and then lay back behind the beat on the next measure. The trumpet player uses dynamics within the solo to invoke a feeling. The trumpet player will use his or her instrument in the same way you are using your voice, except without the lyrics. However, one of the most amazing things about jazz is the voice it gives to each instrument in an ensemble. All players have equal opportunity to evoke emotions in the audience.

INFLUENTIAL SINGERS

In order to continue the jazz tradition and honor the idiom, it is important to hear who came before us and how they found unique approaches
to improvisation. Not all jazz singers improvise using scat. Some jazz
vocalists utilize wordless vocals emulating jazz instrumentalists instead
of lyrics. Some improvise with phrasing. When we find a vocalist that
touches us with his or her unique sound, we may be attracted to the
quality of the voice, the expression of the musical accompaniment, or
the groove or beat of the song. After some time cultivating your jazz
listening, you may notice that the singers you like today may actually
sound like some of the blues and jazz singers of the past. This may not
be obvious at first. But, as the way you musically listen develops, you
may find that how a certain vocalist phrases or the approach to a song
is not as original as you thought. Try to listen beyond the arrangement.
Listen to the voice, the phrasing, the emotion and feeling, and the vocal
delivery. For example, listen to Sister Rosetta Thorpe and then listen to
early recordings of Aretha Franklin. Don't listen for the quality of vocal
tone to be the same, but focus on listening to the approach, the articulation and phrasing, and the overall use of the voice.

Several years back, pop singer Christina Aguilera recorded the song
"I Got Trouble." She used an older-style rhythm section as accompaniment, and she also used studio effects on the track to make the band and
voice sound like an old recording. Listen to this recording by Christina
Aguilera and then compare this to Bessie Smith's version of "Downhearted Blues." Although Christina Aguilera is not a jazz singer, you can
hear blues and rhythm and blues influence in her vocal delivery. ♪

Frank Sinatra

To some, Frank Sinatra would be considered a crooner or a pop
singer. To others, he could be thought of as a jazz singer. Either way,
we do know that Frank Sinatra in his early career was influenced by
both jazz and cabaret singers. Sinatra did not scat, but he did improvise
rhythmically. You can hear this especially in his 1940s and 1950s recordings. When singing a ballad, Frank Sinatra had the gift of a heartfelt
delivery that caused the listener to feel the emotion and meaning of the

lyrics. At the height of his career, his phraseology, much like Billie Holi-day, was impressive, and he held on to notes across the bar line for em-phasis. Sinatra had great breath control—he could sing a phrase softly while holding on to a word or note. He could also sing a phrase while gradually getting louder at the peak of the phrase, holding the note out.

Sinatra was a master interpreter. His rhythmic sense was excellent, and his ability to make an audience feel the emotion in a song was outstanding. Every inflection of the lyrics was also a part of his song interpretation. Throughout Sinatra's career, he sang songs from the American Songbook. However, by the late 1960s, Sinatra also delved into contemporary popular music. Sinatra interspersed popular music into his later career performances. In fact, younger audiences who heard Sinatra singing later in his life related more to his popular record-ing of songs like "New York, New York" and "My Way."

Called the Chairman of the Board by musicians and friends, Sinatra had command of every song he performed. His phrasing and articula-tion was that of a jazz singer. His ability to emote within a song touched the heart of many who heard him, both on recordings and in live per-formances. Listen to the rhythmic phrasing of Frank Sinatra on Cole Porter's "Just One of those Things" (*Frank Sinatra Sings for Young Lovers*) (figures 5.2a and 5.2b). ♪

There are many recordings by Frank Sinatra. The song "If You Are But a Dream," released as a single 78 version, is a good example of how Frank Sinatra sounded during his early career. "Guess I'll Hang My Tears Out to Dry," "Pennies from Heaven," "Only the Lonely," and "I Won't Dance" also offer excellent examples of Sinatra's rhythmic phrasing. ♪

Jimmy Scott

When you first hear Jimmy Scott sing, you will be surprised that you are listening to a man and not a woman. Due to a rare genetic condition, he was born with a slight build and a voice much higher than most men—hence the nickname Little Jimmy Scott, which was given to him by Lionel Hampton, his bandleader for many years. He sang with an unusually high contralto voice, which gives him a unique place in the jazz idiom. When he recorded "Embraceable You" with Charlie Parker, the credit was mistakenly given to a female singer! Scott's phrasing and interpretation were unique and engaged the listener emotionally. He did not follow the

Figure 5.2a. Original Rhythm of "Just One of Those Things." *From* High Society. *Words and Music by Cole Porter* ©*1935 (Renewed) WB Music Corp. All Rights Reserved.*

JUST ONE OF THOSE THINGS
As recorded by Frank Sinatra (1950–1954)

Transcr. by D. Schachter

Figure 5.2b.   Frank Sinatra's Interpretation of "Just One of Those Things."
D. Schachter

original written rhythm of the songs he sang but used his own musical instincts in his improvised phrasing to his story.

Little known during his early years, Jimmy Scott dropped out of the music business only to emerge later in life. However, he was always a singer's singer, admired by legends such as Billie Holiday, Dinah Washington, and Nancy Wilson for his romantic, expressive interpretations of songs. Scott's interpretive skills and rhythmic phrasing are characteristic of the best jazz singing. He also represents a singer who truly found his own voice, even though it was a highly unusual voice for a man. He embraced the fact that his voice was different than the normal male voice of the time and worked with the vocal tool he was given to hone his craft. Listen to Jimmy Scott's recordings "Address Unknown" and "Imagination." ♪

Carmen McRae

Before Carmen McRae became one of the most influential vocalists of the twentieth century, she played piano and worked as a secretary in New York. Deeply influenced by Billie Holiday, she came to the attention of producers in the late 1930s while working in a New York club. She recognized that Holiday was very ahead of her time and built upon her influence as she developed her own style. You can truly hear Billie Holiday's influence in McRae's live recording of "It's Like Reaching for the Moon." ♪

Carmen McRae had a way with words as she sang. She was known less for the technical prowess of her voice than for her deeply skillful phrasing and intonation. Like Billie Holiday, she could hold on to a word or note for emphasis. A specific inflection or subtle use of an accent added to her song interpretation. She would scoop up to a word and pause, which felt like she was letting the audience in on a conversation, telling us her story. Her phrasing was very conversational. McRae used laid-back phrasing while subtly making use of gradual dynamics. Her timing within a phrase was impeccable. Even when McRae's voice dropped from a higher-toned voice to a lower register as she got older, her improvisational phrasing continued to develop. In medium up-tempo songs, McRae would sometimes scat but most often would improvise a melody with the lyrics as in her recording of "Sometimes I'm Happy" originally recorded on Decca Records. Listen to the 1973 recording of McRae singing "All the Things You Are" for additional examples of her phrasing and delivery. ♪

Bing Crosby

Like Carmen McRae, Bing Crosby did not start as a singer, but as a drummer. When Crosby was very young, he already had an innate talent for rhythm. After he and his longtime bandmate Al Rinker spent time in a band in which he played drums, they left and formed the Rhythm Boys with Harry Barris, a third vocalist. The trio came up with a unique act, singing in harmony while Barris played piano. The three emulated the sounds of instruments, horns to drum, and cymbal sounds. For effect, Barris would be playing the piano and then stop and slam the top of the upright piano, making the sound of a cymbal with his mouth. Rinker sang the higher voice, Barris the middle, and Crosby the low part. Crosby would take most of the solo parts while the other two men would sing background parts in scat or imitate instruments. The earliest recordings of the Rhythm Boys go back to 1927.

During this time period, Crosby honed his singing skills. He left the Rhythm Boys in 1931, and throughout the 1930s, he was the most celebrated and influential singer in America. Since his talent was developed before the age of microphones, singers who belted out songs such as Al Jolson and Sophie Tucker did not as strongly influence Crosby. Bing Crosby's affiliation was with jazz. In his early solo singing, he effortlessly slid into notes, would bend notes within a phrase, and incorporated jazz hornlike phrases and some scat phrases. As time went on, record producers encouraged Bing Crosby not to sound too "jazzy," and his style evolved with the times. His career spanned almost fifty years, and he was a major star, bringing his style to millions of people across America. He recorded more than one thousand songs, was a popular radio star, hosted television shows, and was an actor and singer in film. Bing Crosby was one of the white singers in the 1920s that was influenced by Louis Armstrong's trumpet and vocal phrasing and improvisation. Crosby's singing helped bring early jazz style to the attention of American audiences and influenced many singers who came after him. To hear the early jazz influence in Bing Crosby's singing, listen to the following recordings:

- *Bing Crosby and Some Jazz Friends*,
- *Bing Crosby, Jazz Singer 1931–1941*, and
- *Timeless Historical Presents Bing Crosby 1926–1932* (especially "Mississippi Mud"). ♪

Sarah Vaughan

Sarah Vaughan grew up in a musically inclined family in Newark, New Jersey, during the 1920s and 1930s. She started piano lessons at the age of seven. When Sarah Vaughan was about eighteen years old, she and a friend went to Amateur Night at the Apollo in New York City. She coaxed her friend to sing with Vaughan accompanying her on piano. Vaughan decided to go back to another Amateur Night at the Apollo and sing, hoping to win the prize. Vaughan won a ten-dollar prize and a week to perform at the Apollo. Sometime in 1943, Sarah Vaughan met jazz pianist Earl "Fatha" Hines, who asked her to join his band. Vaughan eventually started her career as a solo artist in 1945 and began performing in New York City nightclubs.

Sarah Vaughan's voice was unlike other vocalists. The timbre of her voice was more full-bodied. As she grew older, her voice became even richer. She could slide from one vocal register to another easily, from a full, deep sound to a light, airy sound. Her phrasing was often conversational, adding specific articulation to some of the lyrics for emphasis that drew in the listener. She scatted effortlessly as if it were all a part of the original song. Her vocal tone had a natural vibrato that she used at the end of her phrases. Sometimes she would use her voice and her vibrato to color the words of the song or to emulate a horn sound. Vaughan would make her vibrato fast or slow according to her own unique interpretation with lyrics or in scatting. She had legendary control over her instrument.

Try listening to Sarah Vaughan in her early career and then in her mid- and later career. You will hear the development of Sarah Vaughan from a big band singer as a young woman to one of the most recognized jazz vocalists of all time. Listen to the following albums:

- *Sarah Vaughan Young Sassy* and
- *Sarah Vaughan at Mr. Kelly's.*

Mel Tormé

Singer Mel Tormé was multitalented—in addition to singing, he was also an actor, writer, composer, arranger, and drummer. Mel Tormé started his own vocal group in 1944, the Mel-Tones, but by 1947 he went solo. In some circles and biographies, Tormé is considered a pop singer. His smooth singing on ballads gave him the nickname the Velvet Fog. However, all it takes is to listen to some of his scat solos to understand that he was in fact a masterful jazz singer. His scat solos on medium and up-tempo songs were beyond compare, nearly matching his idol Ella Fitzgerald. His smooth, gentle delivery exhibited clever rhythmic complexity and interpretation. Examples of Mel Tormé's singing include:

- "Lullaby of Birdland,"
- "Sent For You Yesterday and Here You Come Today,"
- "Hi –Fly," and
- "It Don't Mean a Thing." ♪

INFLUENTIAL VOCAL GROUPS

The Boswell Sisters

The Boswell sisters were raised in New Orleans in the 1910s and 1920s. Both Connie Boswell and her work with her sisters, The Boswell Sisters, influenced vocal groups and jazz soloists long after they retired. The Boswell Sisters were a self-contained group with Martha Boswell on piano and vocals and Helvetia and Connie Boswell on vocals. The sisters were known for singing in intricate harmonies. By the time the sisters were first recorded with a remote recording in 1928, they were not only harmonizing but also imitating horns. The sisters intertwined their "horns" in between the song lyrics. Their arrangements were unique in that they often added modulations into popular songs of the time, starting off in one key and then switching to a different key, sometimes from major to minor or vice versa. They added similar variations rhythmically. Often they would begin with one rhythmic groove, but then would slow the next section down, returning again to a fast tempo during the last half of the song. Even though many of the sisters' recordings from 1931 to 1936 included horn players such as Glen Miller, Manny Klein, and Benny Goodman, they often performed as a trio. During their live performances, the sisters took even more musical risks by breaking a song tempo, dropping into a slower tempo, and adding to the original melody of a song within the arrangement. The horn licks were sung in harmony, as were the song lyrics.

The Boswell Sisters influenced other singers with their creative interpretations of songs. Listening to their recordings now, it is easy to hear them as very old-fashioned. However, their harmonic arrangements, rhythmic interpretations, and instrumental singing were considered musically unique during the early 1930s. They were ahead of their time. Examples of The Boswell Sisters' unique harmonies and arrangements include: "Heebie Jeebies," "Shout Sister Shout," "Roll on Mississippi," and "If It Ain't Love." ♪

The Mills Brothers

Like the Boswell Sisters, the Mills Brothers were a family band that grew up singing together. Their early years were spent harmonizing in church. As they developed as singers, they began to use uncannily accurate vocal imitations of horns and other instruments. They were often only accompanied by a guitar but created such a wide variety of sounds—horns, percussion, and bass—that the listener would think an entire band was playing. They also used closely interwoven harmonies along with their instrumental singing. Their rhythm and phrasing was uncanny. The Mills Brothers were the first Black vocal group that grew wide popularity among white audiences, and they profoundly advanced the art of instrumental singing. Suggested listening examples of the Mills Brothers include "Tiger Rag," "St. Louis Blues," and "I Heard."

Lambert, Hendricks & Ross

Jazz vocalists Dave Lambert, Annie Ross, and Jon Hendricks came together in 1957 to create a new vocal trio. Their goal was to sing more like jazz instrumentalists than traditional jazz singers. Their group voicings were considered unusual to general audiences mainly because the song material was instrumentally based, including the group's singing of instrumental solos. To jazz audiences and musicians, they were considered "hip." Lambert, Hendricks & Ross sang bebop, singing in harmony while using open chord voicings and close voicings. They sang and phrased like trumpet and sax players.

Jon Hendricks wrote many of the lyrics for the group's songs. He not only wrote words to the song itself, but often wrote lyrics to the instrumental solo (saxophone or trumpet) as well. Hendricks wrote the lyrics to an instrumental song by Jimmy Giuffre, "Four Brothers." On one recording, by members of the Woody Herman Orchestra, saxophonists Zoot Sims, Stan Getz, Herbie Steward, and Serge Chaloff each take a solo. In the Lambert, Hendricks & Ross version, each singer takes a solo much modeled after those saxophone solos, but with lyrics delivered in the same freely flowing form as an instrumental solo. This form of jazz singing, in which lyrics are delivered in the style of instrumental solos, is called vocalese.

Lambert, Hendricks & Ross took vocal groups to a new level. The sound of the trio and the arrangements influenced many vocal groups up to the present. The lyrics Hendricks wrote to jazz instrumental solos and songs are still performed today. When you listen to Lambert, Hendricks

& Ross, you will notice how difficult the arrangements were and the vocal demands of each vocalist within the trio. Singing instrumental solos is not easy and requires complete control over not only your voice, but also your understanding of where you are in the song, your rhythmic sensitivity, and intonation. Listening examples include:

- "Four Brothers" (recorded on Woody Herman, *The Thundering Herds 1945–1947*, Columbia, 1947 release)
- "Four Brothers" (recorded by Lambert, Hendricks & Ross, *Sing a Song of Basie*, Universal Music Mexico, 1957) ♪

The Manhattan Transfer

No other vocal group since the 1970s has had the impact in vocal jazz and vocal jazz education as The Manhattan Transfer. In many ways, The Manhattan Transfer single-handedly brought jazz back to general audiences who were not familiar with jazz or had been previously disinterested. Combining bebop, novelty songs, and different arrangements of jazz and popular music, The Manhattan Transfer's vocal arrangements reimagined elements of older music, such as close harmonies, vocalese, and scat singing. Influenced by jazz greats Jon Hendricks, Ella Fitzgerald, and many instrumental jazz artists, The Manhattan Transfer revived songs from the 1930s and 1940s. The group has featured jazz vocalists such as Jon Hendricks and Bobby McFerrin and various instrumentalists from the Count Basie Orchestra, bassist Ray Brown, and horn player Dizzy Gillespie, among others. Suggestions for listening include "Sing Joy Spring," "A Night in Tunisia" (featuring Bobby McFerrin), and "Tuxedo Junction." ♪

Bobby McFerrin

One-man bands existed throughout jazz music history in the form of self-contained blues singers who sang, played guitar, and sometimes had a harmonica strapped to their shoulders as an added instrument. Other blues artists and later some jazz pianists added a hi-hat for percussion. For nearly fifty decades in St. Louis, Missouri, saxophonist Hugh "Peanuts" Whalum made his living playing local clubs, parties, and other events as a pianist/singer using a hi-hat cymbal on a stand close to his piano, his foot playing the hi-hat as he played and sang.

Singer Bobby McFerrin is most well known for creating a multi-instrumental sound with only his voice as an instrument in sound and phrasing. He does not use any actual instruments. He is included here because he truly is a one-man band! His voice is the complete instrument, singing bass lines, drumbeats, and cymbals, while also emulating a horn instrument. Utilizing a wide vocal range, including a strong falsetto, McFerrin sings with ease through difficult instrumental passages. McFerrin is also known for his overtone singing, in which he can manipulate the resonance and tone of his voice to sing more than one pitch at a time. This modern version of overtone singing has roots deep in Mongolia—and far away from the origins of jazz—and showcases McFerrin's complete mastery of his voice as an instrument. His vocal acrobatics and creativity are unparalleled in modern jazz.

McFerrin has built upon the influences of legendary jazz singers, such as Ella Fitzgerald (particularly for her improvisational ideas), Lambert, Hendricks & Ross, Eddie Jefferson, and many great jazz instrumentalists such as Miles Davis and Dizzy Gillespie to create a profoundly unique sound and style.

Among McFerrin's CDs, *The Best of Bobby McFerrin* showcases the talents and artistry of McFerrin. On this CD, listen to McFerrin's work on the song "Spain" with jazz pianist Chick Corea, and listen to the song "Freedom Is a Voice" recorded with pianist Russell Ferrante. This same CD also includes McFerrin's popular hit "Don't Worry Be Happy," in which he sings lyrics while vocally jumping up and down registers to sing bass and percussion. Another CD, *Round Midnight*, includes the title track "Round Midnight" (from the 1986 movie of the same name) with McFerrin singing as a horn. ♪

SOUNDING LIKE A JAZZ SINGER: TECHNIQUE AND DELIVERY

Learning to hear jazz differently than other forms of music is an ongoing process. Many aspiring jazz instrumentalists study and learn great jazz artists' styles and improvisational solos. For singers learning the roots of blues and jazz, listening to great jazz vocalists' improvisational solos and phraseology is a great teaching tool. This, of course, is coupled with the vocalist's natural sense of singing, vocal control, and facility of the voice. The other thing to keep in mind when listening to great jazz vocals is to understand one's own unique sound. You can borrow the phrasing and melodic ideas of jazz greats, but it is important to incorporate this within your own natural voice. You don't have to sound exactly like the jazz artist you are emulating to become a jazz singer.

Phraseology

Rhythmic phrasing of jazz singers is unlike any of the other American song idioms such as pop, rock, R&B, or country. In order to phrase like a jazz singer, you need to understand the rhythm and groove of the song. The rhythm of the song is the consistent timing of each measure. The groove is the time-feel as the singer literally floats over the time.

This rhythmic momentum, as Dave Liebman describes in his article "The Saxophone and Related Jazz Topics," "has ramifications about it, whether it is cast in a forward, aggressive manner or a relaxed, laid back sense. One way of describing this feeling is to use the word 'groove' in describing rhythmic momentum."

Liebman further writes, "In jazz after tone, it is what I call 'time-feel' that most expresses an artist's unique conception. The manner in which the player rhythmically phrases is to an even larger degree more revealing than the actual melodic and harmonic content. It conveys a truly physical impression to the listener, which is difficult to describe in words."

Rhythmic phrasing is a large element of jazz improvisation. Jazz singers can lay back behind the beat or change the rhythm of each phrase. Listen again to jazz vocalist Billie Holiday's phrasing. She has such finesse with rhythmic phrasing that you may not notice that her phrasing is usually not the original rhythm of the song.

Melodic Improvisation

For the singer, melodic improvisation can occur when singing the lyrics of a song or singing scat syllables to a song. When you hear jazz singers improvise, such as Ella Fitzgerald scatting, they are altering the melody of the song, and in essence creating a countermelody that matches the chord progressions of the song. This is a skill that takes time to develop. During the 1940s and 1950s, musicians worked several times a week or more. Audiences came to see and hear jazz. Singers had the opportunity to work alongside great instrumentalists, who would always take solos during the set.

The program of songs was basically the same from night to night, adding a new song or two within a time frame usually set by the bandleader. This meant that the vocalist would listen to the same song and improvised solos of the horn players, guitar, and piano. This repetition helped to solidify the melody and chord progressions of the song for the vocalist.

Often the inexperienced singer may listen to a singer like Ella Fitzgerald, Anita O'Day, or Mel Tormé's improvisational scat lines and think that scat singing is effortless and easy—until we try it ourselves! In general the scat singers have technical command of their voices. They have a considerable vocal range with enough vocal control to slide up and down the scale with ease. These singers also have a good sense of jazz harmony. They hear the chord progressions of a standard jazz song and improvise on the spot.

How can you learn how to scat? To reiterate once more, listen to many jazz greats, both instrumentalists and vocalists. Try to isolate the band to sing back the rhythm of the drums. Try to sing all the parts of the drums, the bass drum beat, the ride cymbal, and other rhythmic nuances you hear the drummer playing. Do the same for the bass. Then listen to the primary chordal instrument (usually piano or guitar). Listen to how she or he plays with the bass and drums. For example, does the pianist play chords on the beat or off the beat? When the pianist or guitarist plays the melody of a song, listen also to the accompanying chords being played. There is, of course, much more to scat singing and improvisation, but this will help you get started. We will explore this skill in more depth over the next few chapters.

Interpretation

The way a jazz singer interprets a song includes rhythmic and melodic improvisation. But interpretation also involves vocal delivery, use of dynamics, vocal inflections, and expression. The jazz singer is an interpreter of the music and the lyrics—the storyteller. The singer's own unique voice and delivery, melodic and rhythmic improvisation, dynamics, and vocal inflections all add to the song interpretation. Much like a person who is reading a poem, the meaning of the words often depends upon the person who is speaking to us. Jazz singers may touch us with their pure melodic sense and phrasing, intensity of emotion, and dynamics or vocal agility coupled with improvisational skills. Any and all contribute to the interpretation. Yet underneath the vocal interpretation, the jazz singer's foundation lies in impeccable rhythm and timing sense, knowing the original melody and how it fits with the chord progressions of the song. Early jazz players and singers used their natural musical instincts to create a musical experience. The steps necessary for aspiring jazz singers to develop strong musicianship are:

- Listen, listen, and listen to jazz greats—both instrumentalists and vocalists.
- Listen to the horn solos as well as the vocalist solos, and pay particular attention to the soloists and how the solo fits in with the music.
- Pay attention to the rhythm that the bass and drummer play.
- Learn the blues scale.
- Work on jazz repertoire, and learn the original melody first.
- Try singing with the jazz soloist you hear on a recording.

Choose one artist at a time to listen to, and listen to the artist's recordings from different time periods starting from the early years. In addition, you can find *Music Minus One* CDs so that you can sing along with a rhythm section for practice. If possible, learn basic keyboard skills to help your overall musicianship.

For example, consider listening to "September in the Rain" (Sarah Vaughn and her Trio, *At Mr. Kelly's, Chicago*, Verve, 1957). ♪

Key: A section refers to the verses within a jazz standard. B section refers to the bridge of middle of the song that has a different melody than the verses. Introduction into the song: Piano starts out playing the first four measures. On the fifth measure he leads the band (bass and drums) in an easy swing tempo for four more measures, leading the vocalist into the song. A section: Song verse. Sarah Vaughan sings through the first A section.

Compare the rhythmic phrasing that Sarah is singing in relationship to the lead sheet. She often comes in on the "and" of beat one.
She emphasizes some specific words as in "That September" by holding on to the note/word "that." In the B section, Sarah Vaughan sings
the bridge of the song beginning with the words "To every word." In
the A section, the vocal returns to the verse, which is the last eight
bars of the song. Turn Around: The pianist plays two measures that
lead the vocalist back into the top of the song, the verse. In the second
A section, Sarah improvises melodically and rhythmically while singing the lyrics. During the last four bars, the bass is playing the same
accents as the pianist on beat one and three. Second B section: Sarah
continues her improvised solo with lyrics. In the last A section, the
improvised solo continues with Sarah singing the last phrase, "September in the Rain." Ending: Sarah elongates the ending, repeating

Figure 5.3a. "September in the Rain" Sheet Music Edition.
Words by Al Dubin, Music by Harry Warren © 1937 (Renewed) WB
Music Corp. All Rights Reserved.

SEPTEMBER IN THE RAIN

Figure 5.3b. "September in the Rain" Lead Sheet. *Words by Al Dubin, Music by Harry Warren.*

the phrase two more times. Because she repeats this last section of the song three times, we call this a "tag" ending.

BIBLIOGRAPHY

Atkins, B. (1925). Heebie jeebies. As recorded by the Boswell Sisters. *Boswell Sisters and Connie Boswell* [CD]. Living Era. 1994.

Austin, L., & Hunter, A. (1922). Downhearted blues. *Bessie Smith Greatest Hits*. Acrobat Records. (2005).

Basie, E., Rushing, J., & Durham, E. (1938). Sent for you yesterday and here you come today. As recorded by Mel Tormé. *Mel Tormé Best of the Concord Years* [CD]. Concord Records. (1999).

Burke, J., and Johnson, A. (1936). Pennies from heaven. *Songs for Swingin' Lovers Frank Sinatra* [CD]. Capitol Records. (1998).

Ellington, D. (1939). In a mellow tone. As recorded by Helen Merrill. *The Duets: Helen Merrill and Ron Carter*. Universal Classics Records. (1989).

Ellington, D., & Mills, I. (1931). It don't mean a thing if it ain't got that swing. As recorded by Mel Tormé. *Mel Tormé with Ray Anthony and His Big Band Live At The Playboy Jazz Festival*. Playboy Jazz. (2002).

Gershwin, G., & Gershwin, I. (1930). But not for me. *Prince of Cool: The Pacific Jazz Years*. (1952–1957).

Gershwin, G., & Gershwin, I. (1928). Embraceable you. *One Night in Birdland* [CD]. Sony Records. (1993).

Gershwin, G., & Gershwin, I. (1930 /1945). I got rhythm/Anthropology. As recorded by Sheila Jordan. *Songs from Within*. MA Recordings. (2008).

Green, J., Heyman, E., Sour, R., & Eyton, F. (1930). Body and soul. *Little Jimmy Scott Regal Records Live in New Orleans* [CD]. Specialty. (1991).

Jaffe, M., Bonx, N., & Fulton, J. (1941). If you are but a dream. *The Essential Frank Sinatra*. Sony Legacy. (2010).

Jones, I. (1936). There is no greater love. *Paul Chambers Three Classic Albums* [CD]. Mischief Records. (2010).

Kern, J., & Hammerstein II, O. (1939). All the things you are. *Chet Baker in Paris*. Disc. 2. EmArcy-837475-2. (1988).

Kern, J., & Hammerstein II, O. (1939). All the things you are. *Carmen McRae: Velvet Soul*. LRC Jazz Classics. Groove. Merchant. (2005).

Kern, J., Hammerstein II, O., & Harbach, O. (1934). I won't dance. *Sinatra-Basie* [CD]. Reprise. (1999).

LaRocca, N., Edwards, E., Ragas, H., Sbarbaro, T., & Shields, L. (1917). DaCosta, H. (1931). As recorded by The Mills Brothers. *Classic Tunes with the Mills Brothers* [CD]. X5 Music Group. (2008).

Lewis, M., & Hamilton N. (1940). How high the moon. *Charlie Parker and Ella Fitzgerald. Charlie Parker: Jazz At the Philharmonic 1949 (Live)*. Verve Music Group.

Liebman, D. (2010). The saxophone and related jazz topics. *Dave Liebman on Education*. Jamey Aebersold Jazz.

McRae, Carmen. Montreal Concert. 1988 excerpt from live concert.

Mercer, J., & Van Heusen, J. (1939). I thought about you. *Some of my Best Friends Are Singers, Ray Brown Trio*. Telarc Records. (1998).

Mundy, J., & Mercer, J. (1943). Travelin' light. As recorded by Sachal Vasandani. *We Move: Sachal Vasadani*. Mack Records [CD]. (2009).

Oliver, S. (1940). Easy does it. *Soluar Energy: The Ray Brown Trio*. Concord. (1984).

Parker C. (1945). Ornithology. *Charlie Parker—Best of the Complete Savoy and Dial Studio Recordings*. SLG LLG. (Savoy Records. 1944–1948). (2002).

Parker, C., & Gillespie, D. (1945). Anthropology. *"Bird" Charlie Parker (1949 Concert and All Stars) 1950–51* [CD]. Fortune Records. (1981).

Parker, C., & Gillespie, D. (1945). Anthropology. *Evolution: Kitty Margolis*. Mad-Kat Records. (1994).

Parker, C., & Gillespie, D. (1945). Anthropology. As recorded by Sheila Jordan. *Sheila Jordan Lost and Found*. Muse Records. (1990).

Perry, L., & Aguilera, C. (2006). I got trouble. *Back to Basics: Christina Aguilera*. RCA Records.

Petterson, O. (1989). Kelly's blues. *Don't Get Sassy: The Ray Brown Trio*. Telarc. (1994).

Porter, C. (1935). Just one of those things. *Frank Sinatra Songs for Young Lovers* [CD]. Capitol Records. (1955).

Shearing, G., & Weiss, G. D. (1952). Lullaby of birdland. As recorded by Mel Tormé. *Mel Tormé Lullaby of Birdland* [CD]. Dynamic Records. (2008).

Sherman, A., Marqusee, G., & Lewis, A. (1936). It's like reaching for the moon. *Carmen McRae in concert*. Montreal. (1988).

Styne, J., & Cahn. S. (1945). Guess I'll hang my tears out to dry. *The Essential Frank Sinatra*. Columbia Records. (2010).

Van Heusen, J., & Burke, J. (1940). Imagination. *Savoy Jazz Super EP: Jimmy Scott* [CD]. Specialty. (1999).

Van Heusen, J., & Cahn, S. (1955). Only the lonely. *Frank Sinatra Sings Only the Lonely*. Capitol Records. (1998).

Various. (1990). *Intimate Ella* [CD]. Verve. (1960).

Various. (1996). *Ella Fitzgerald and the Tommy Flanagan Trio* [CD]. Laser-light.

Various. (2004). *The Swingin's Mutual George Shearing Quintet with Nancy Wilson* [CD]. Capitol Records. (1960).

Waller, T., Razaf, A., & Redman, D. (1931). If it ain't love. As recorded by the Boswell Sisters. *Shout Sister Shout! 1925–1936: The Boswell Sisters* [CD]. Jazz Legends. (2004).

Warren H., & Dubin, A. (1934). I heard oh yes I heard. As recorded by the Mills Brothers. *The Mills Brothers 1931–34*. Giants of Jazz. (1992).

Weston, R., (1954) & Hendricks, J. (1961). Hi-fly. As recorded by Mel Tormé. *Mel Tormé Best of the Concord Years* [CD]. Concord Records. (1999).

Williams, C. (1929). Shout sister shout. As recorded by the Boswell Sisters. *Shout Sisters Shout! 1925–1936: The Boswell Sisters* [CD]. Jazz Legends. (2004).

6

THE GREAT
AMERICAN SONGBOOK

The Great American Songbook, contrary to its name, isn't a physical book. Rather, this refers to the canon of songs that are considered the most influential and important popular songs of the twentieth century, particularly from the 1920s through the 1950s. These songs are an important part of jazz repertoire. As a jazz singer, listening to and knowing these songs is essential.

The Great American Songbook is a phenomenon and includes many songs we refer to today as "jazz standards," which means that they are standard songs for jazz singers and instrumentalists to know by rote. These songs are still played and recognized today, despite their being written as far back as the 1920s. The songwriters wrote heartfelt, clever, and humorous lyrics that are still relatable many years later. During the time when these songs were written—approximately between the 1920s and 1950s—there was a plethora of performance venues in the country, particularly in larger cities. Songs were written for the Broadway and music theater stage, films, big bands, and vocalists. In no other time period were so many songs grouped together in this way. The musical arrangements of these standard songs are played today in many different formats, including traditional jazz bands, contemporary arrangements with more diverse instrumentation, and R&B and funk arrangements.

In general, jazz musicians are expected to know these standards. The Great American Songbook music is still recorded by up-and-coming jazz instrumentalists and vocalists to showcase their chops.

THE GREAT AMERICAN SONGWRITERS

There are far too many talented and prolific songwriters to include a full accounting in this chapter. However, there are a few standouts that are worth exploring in some depth. For each song and songwriter (or songwriters) mentioned, you will be overwhelmed by the amount of available recordings to explore. These songs have been recorded and re-recorded since their initial debuts. Enjoy your explorations! .

George and Ira Gershwin

George and Ira Gershwin were brothers born into a Russian Jewish immigrant family in New York City in the late 1800s. George was the more musical of the two and secretly learned how to play piano during his early teens. In 1914 he left high school to become a song plugger on Tin Pan Alley, the name given to the section of New York City that, at the time, was dominated by music publishers. During the early 1900s, popular music was primarily disseminated through sheet music. Song pluggers were essentially hired guns who would play songs for customers shopping for sheet music, so they would be able to hear the song before their purchase. George was immersed in the popular music of the era as he worked in this environment, and this greatly influenced his compositions.

Ira was the more studious of the two brothers and began publishing light verse in newspapers while he studied at the College of New York. George was already gaining recognition for his songwriting when he and Ira began their incredible collaboration, which resulted in more than twenty scores for both theater and film. Ira's lyrics are still considered the gold standard for American popular song and continue to provide songwriters of today with inspiration and education. George's musical compositions combine a deep interest in modern classical composers, such as Maurice Ravel, Dmitri Shostakovich, and Arnold Schoenberg, with a love of the jazz and popular music he was immersed in while working on Tin Pan Alley. Together, the Gershwins were committed to writing music that reflected the here and now of American life.

Listening recommendations from the Gershwins' repertoire include: "I Love You Porgy," "Summertime," "Our Love is Here to Stay," "I Got Rhythm," "Someone to Watch Over Me," "Embraceable You," "Who Cares," "But Not for Me," "A Foggy Day," and "I've Got a Crush on You." ♪

Cole Porter

Cole Porter was born an only son into a wealthy Indiana family in 1891. He learned violin and piano at an early age. He went to Yale for college. While he majored in English, he wrote more than three hundred songs and was involved in the Yale Glee Club, and music was his primary activity. He went to Harvard Law School after Yale, at the behest of his grandfather, but later secretly transferred to the music department. After college he had a mixed record of Broadway songwriting success in New York City before moving to Paris around 1917. While in Paris, he continued to write for Broadway but also studied classical orchestration and counterpoint.

Porter's first major Broadway success came in 1928 with the musical *Paris*. This was followed by a string of successful shows, including *Anything Goes* and *Kiss Me, Kate*, which are still performed today. Porter was active on Broadway and in Hollywood up until the late 1950s, and while his career was at its zenith in the 1930s, many of his later songs also became standards. Porter's educational background and time in Paris lent his lyrics and music a sophisticated air, but his sense of humor shines through—all it takes is a quick listen to "Anything Goes" to get a sense of Porter's wit.

Listening recommendations from Porter's repertoire include: "Let's Do It, Let's Fall in Love," "I Concentrate on You," "I Got You Under My Skin," "Ev'ry Time We Say Goodbye," "Night and Day," and "All of You." ♪

Irving Berlin

It is nearly impossible to overstate the importance of Irving Berlin's contributions to the Great American Songbook. Over his incredibly long, prolific career, which spanned from around 1907 all the way to the early 1960s, he wrote an estimated 1,500 songs. Some of his most famous songs are songs you are intimately familiar with already, such as "White Christmas" (the best-selling song of all time) and "God Bless America." Irving Berlin was born in Russia in 1888, during a time when Jews were being brutally persecuted, and his family escaped to America when he was five years old. His early life was spent in abject poverty in the slums of New York City; his father, who had been a cantor (a singer in a synagogue who leads the congregation in prayer) in Russia but struggled to find work in America, died when he was thirteen years old. Irving and his sisters had to find odd jobs to support the family. Young Berlin eventually started singing on the streets for small change. A completely self-taught musician, he eventually worked as a song plugger in Union Square and also sang and played at various saloons, where he discovered a knack for making up funny songs to entertain the customers. He was discovered by a staff member at a music publishing firm and took a job as a staff lyricist in 1909, around the age of twenty-one—in spite of being able to compose songs in only one key! ♪

In 1911 he had his first hit with "Alexander's Ragtime Band," which reinvigorated the national craze for ragtime for American and international audiences. From 1911 until the end of his career, Irving Berlin wrote hit after hit for both Broadway and Hollywood. In spite of his obvious genius, he always maintained that all of his success was due only to hard work and focus! He composed a wide variety of songs in many styles, including dance songs, patriotic songs, and ballads. Like his contemporaries, his focus was on writing songs that the public could embrace and appreciate, with a focus on catchy melodies and simple, accessible lyrics. This focus on accessibility and simplicity is what makes his songs so timeless—can you imagine a holiday season without "White Christmas"? ♪

Listening recommendations from Berlin's repertoire include "Change Partners," "Blue Skies," "Always," "Cheek to Cheek," "How Deep is the Ocean?" "Let's Face the Music and Dance," "Supper Time," and "What'll I Do?" ♪

Duke Ellington

Duke Ellington was born in 1899 in Washington, D.C. Both parents were pianists and insisted that he learn, though he didn't show an immediate affinity for music. He didn't get serious about music until his midteens, when he was exposed to ragtime, which was the popular music of the time and played in bars and poolrooms. He worked hard not only to mimic ragtime pianists but also to polish his technical chops, sight-reading abilities, and music theory knowledge. By his late teens he was playing gigs in clubs around D.C. He made the decision in his early twenties to relocate to Harlem. This first trip led to disappointment. However, he and his early bandmates eventually made it back a few years later, and Ellington's career as a bandleader took off.

Ellington was a master of the three-minute song form and combined elements of ragtime, the blues, and classical European traditions to create a unique sound. He was famous not only in America and gained international acclaim. His career as a well-respected and wildly admired Black composer and bandleader broke ground for other Black artists, and his band provided a platform for many famous soloists. He wrote nearly two thousand songs during his long career.

Listening recommendations from Ellington's repertoire include "It Don't Mean a Thing (If It Ain't Got That Swing)," "In a Sentimental Mood," "Take the 'A' Train," "Mood Indigo," and "I Got It Bad and That Ain't Good." ♪

Harry Warren

Harry Warren, following a similar pattern to many of his contemporaries, was born into an Italian immigrant family in 1893 in Brooklyn, New York. He was one of eleven siblings. His parents could not afford music lessons in spite of their son's interest, but he taught himself to play the family accordion and sang in the church choir. In his midteens, he dropped out of school to play drums for a traveling carnival band led by his godfather. He eventually taught himself piano as well, in between odd jobs. He landed a low-level job at a Brooklyn-based movie studio called Vitagraph Studios and shortly afterward joined the Navy. He started songwriting in earnest while he was in the Navy, and after his time in the armed forces, he became a song plugger on Tin Pan Alley (again, a common theme for Great American Songbook composers!).

In 1929, Warren left the East Coast for southern California and began his prolific film-composing career. His music was eventually in more than three hundred films. The twenty years between 1930 and 1950 were the golden age of movie musicals, and Warren's songs featured prominently. He wrote for several different studios during this time and was nominated for eleven Academy Awards for film music, winning three. While Warren isn't a typical household name, his songs speak for themselves as an important contribution to the Great American Songbook.

Listening recommendations from Warren's repertoire include "I Only Have Eyes for You," "At Last," The More I See You," "There Will Never Be Another You," "You'll Never Know," "Lullaby of Birdland," "I Had the Craziest Dream," "Chattanooga Choo Choo," and "That's Amore." ♪

Harold Arlen

Harold Arlen, born in Buffalo, New York, in 1905, is another prolific and famous composer who doesn't have the name recognition of the Gershwins of the world. However, you've probably heard of a little film called *The Wizard of Oz*—Arlen wrote the music! Before that massive hit, for which he won an Oscar, Arlen spent his early career working as a pianist, vocalist, and accompanist, bouncing between Buffalo and New York City. He got a minor role in a Broadway show in the late 1920s but shifted from acting to accompanying, arranging, and eventually composing songs. He met lyricist Ted Koehler around 1930 or so and began writing melodies for Koehler's lyrics. Their initial hits included songs "Get Happy" and "Stormy Weather." The pair ventured out to Hollywood and started a long and fruitful career writing film musicals, starting with *Let's Fall in Love* in 1933.

In 1939, Arlen wrote the music for *The Wizard of Oz*, which cemented his already excellent reputation in Hollywood. Arlen, much like Warren, wrote famous songs that launched the careers of others much more visibly than their own (Judy Garland, for example). His songs remain popular with jazz performers today for their blues sensibilities and beautiful melodic structure.

Listening recommendations from Arlen's repertoire include "Get Happy," "Let's Fall in Love," "Blues in the Night," "That Old Black Magic," "Stormy Weather," and "One for My Baby (and One More for the Road)." ♪

Women Composers and the Great American Songbook

You may have noticed the composers in the above list have something in common: they are all men. During much of the twentieth century, opportunities for women in jazz were limited outside of the role of the vocalist. Female jazz instrumentalists and composers had a difficult time breaking through the mainstream, in spite of their talent. However, there are several women with standards in the canon that deserve special mention.

Dorothy Fields worked in Hollywood from 1930 to 1939 and wrote "I'm in the Mood for Love" and "Dinner at Eight." She collaborated with Jerome Kern on the song "The Way You Look Tonight," which earned them an Oscar in 1936. She wrote the lyrics for the 1959 musical *Redhead*, which was nominated for seven Tony Awards and won five. ♪

Billie Holiday, along with her phenomenal singing career, cowrote several jazz standards, including "Lady Sings the Blues" and "God Bless the Child," among others.

Dana Suesse was an extremely accomplished pianist, composer, and lyricist who wrote "My Silent Love," "You Ought to Be in Pictures," and "Ho-Hum."

Kay Swift was educated at what is now the Juilliard School of Music in classical composition and was the first woman to completely score a hit musical: *Fine and Dandy* in 1930. She was also a longtime collaborator of George Gershwin before his death in 1937 and assisted Ira in arranging his works posthumously.

SONG CHARACTERISTICS OF THE GREAT AMERICAN SONGBOOK

Structure

Jazz standards almost all follow the same or similar forms. They are generally around three minutes long and follow a thirty-two-bar format, usually structured as AABA or ABAC, with a great deal of variation within these initial structures. The A section establishes the melody, and the B section, or bridge, changes the melody before returning the song to its original verse. The C section could be a second bridge or reinterpreted arrangement of the original A verse.

Lyrics in Great American Songbook songs tend toward the universal and are mostly love songs (which is obvious from their titles). This universality means they can be performed in many different situations. In fact, songs were often written for one movie and performed later in a different play, or vice versa, or revived again later in a different context.

The basic song form from the American Songbook era is: verse (or verses), bridge (B section), verse. Other song forms that differed from this include composers Oscar Levant and Edward Heyman's "Blame It on My Youth," written in 1934, and "I Got Right to Sing the Blues," written by Harold Arlen and Ted Koehler in 1932.

While the form of the songs tended to be the same, the tempos, groove, and feel of the songs differed. Four examples are medium tempo swing, up tempo swing, ballads, and bossa nova. See the listening examples below.

Medium Tempo Swing

Moderate swing tunes were danceable but notably more relaxed than their up tempo brethren. This is the most common tempo demarcation for songs in the Great American Songbook. Moderate swing tunes have a tempo around 120–140 bpm.

Listening recommendations in a medium tempo swing include "Our Love Is Here To Stay," "But Not for Me," "I Got You Under My Skin," "Night and Day," "Time After Time," "The Song Is You," "A Foggy Day," "Take the 'A' Train," "I'm Beginning to See the Light," "Ain't Misbehavin," and "All of Me." ♪

Up Tempo Swing

Faster swing tunes have a tempo around 200–245 bpm. These have a brighter and more upbeat feel than medium tempo swing tunes.

Listening recommendations with an up tempo swing include "In a Mellow Tone," "How High the Moon," and "The Lady Is a Tramp." ♪

Ballads

Ballads are slower, more melancholy songs performed with a smooth delivery and are almost always love songs.

Listening recommendations among ballads include "I've Got a Crush on You," "I Got It Bad and That Ain't Good," "Someone to Watch Over Me," "Tenderly," "Body and Soul," "Loverman," and "Stormy Weather." ♪

Bossa Nova

Rhythmically related to samba (a Brazilian musical genre characterized by a 2/4 tempo), bossa nova songs feature a different rhythmic arrangement than most standard jazz repertoire, with a Latin clave percussion pattern, which is a five-stroke rhythmic pattern using the clave, a traditional percussion instrument consisting of two small wooden cylinders. While not all songs literally use a clave, the rhythm is based on that pattern.

Bossa nova listening recommendations include "The Girl from Ipanema," "Night and Day," "Midnight Sun," and "Quiet Nights and Quiet Stars (Corcovado)." ♪

Arrangements

When you look at a lead sheet for any of the Great American Songbook tunes, they are often marked as tempo "medium swing." However, this should always just be taken as a suggestion. One reason these songs endure is because they are so versatile. An instrumentalist or vocalist can easily reinterpret not only the tempo of these songs but also the arrangement. During the course of your listening explorations, you may have grown attached to certain versions of songs. The old recordings from the 1930s and 1940s tend to have the same traditional big band swing sound. However, different recordings of the same song are worth listening to again and again to get a sense of how different artists of different eras (or even within the same era) reinterpreted these standard songs.

For example, take the song "Just One of Those Things," written in 1935 by Cole Porter. Listen to how different the same song can sound, depending on both the artist and the era in which it was reinterpreted. Everything can be adjusted, from instrumental arrangements to vocal delivery and feel.

Listening recommendations of "Just One of Those Things" featuring a noteworthy arrangement include:

- Frank Sinatra's 1946 ballad interpretation of the song. As recorded by Frank Sinatra, *Sinatra Sings Cole Porter*, Legacy/Columbia, 2003.

- Blossom Dearie's 1957 vibrant double time rhythmic feel behind her easy, relaxed delivery of the same song. As recorded by Blossom Dearie, *Give Him the Ohh-La-La*, Verve, 1999.
- Dee Dee Bridgewater's 1993 fast swing version. As recorded by Dee Dee Bridgewater, *Keeping Tradition*, DDB/Emarcy, 2010.
- Cheryl Bentyne's 2012 version, done as a melancholy rubato ballad with only voice and piano. As recorded by Cheryl Bentyne, *Let's Misbehave: The Cole Porter Songbook*, Summit Records, 2012.

You can take nearly any song from the Great American Songbook and explore different interpretations. Listening to how different artists interpret songs is a large part of developing your own unique jazz sensibilities. The Great American Songbook songs were meant to be played and sung by different artists in different ways—don't be afraid to experiment!

Introductions

Often Great American Songbook songs include an introductory verse sung before the song gets started in earnest, which was often necessary in theater and film settings to provide some context to the actors breaking into song. These introductions may or may not be written out in notation format. For many experienced musicians, an introduction is simply improvised on the spot. Jazz bands may decide to use the last four measures or bars of the song to lead the vocalist into the beginning of the song. However, the introduction can be longer, with added chord progressions that will, toward the end, lead the vocalist into the actual song itself.

Compare the different ways these introductions are interpreted from these recordings of the same song, "But Not for Me" written by George and Ira Gershwin. ♪

- Anita O'Day's leisurely, elegant, 1958 version. As recorded by Anita O'Day, *At Mister Kelly's*, PSP, 2012.
- Chet Baker's 1950s instrumental version. As recorded by Chet Baker, *The Pacific Jazz Years*, Pacific Jazz, 1994.
- Cheryl Bentyne's 2011 version, in which the bassist is using a bow and the drums are playing more of a Latin groove. As recorded by Cheryl Bentyne, *Gershwin Songbook*, Artistshare/CD Baby, 2011.

Endings

Unless there is a specific arrangement written on a lead sheet, the vocalist will have to rely on the band to guide how the song should end. Experienced musicians use their instincts and musical ear, following the pianist or guitarist's chord progression. A vocalist who works with very experienced musicians will often let the rhythm section end the song. However, the vocalist's phrasing toward the end of the song signals to the musicians how and when to end the song. Listen closely to the endings of these recordings:

- Anita O'Day's 1956 version of "Honeysuckle Rose" on her *This is Anita*, Verve, 2012.
- Kenny Rankin's 1991 version of "Someone to Watch Over Me" on his *Because of You*, Chesky, 1991. ♪

Introductions and endings are important in setting up the mood of the song. Specific arrangements can have a great impact on how the audience feels the song.

Modern Reinterpretations

What is notable about the Great American Songbook is that the music of a long-ago era still lives not only in jazz but also in other genres such as R&B and pop. For example, Harry Warren and Al Dubin wrote the song "I Only Have Eyes for You" in 1934. Originally written for a movie, this song has enjoyed perennial success as recorded by a number of different artists in different eras. Listen to the following versions of the song, paying attention to how the time and place of the recording informed the different choices the artists made with regard to arrangement, style, and feel: ♪

- Ben Selvin and his orchestra, as recorded in 1934, *50 Hits: Ben Selvin, The Dean of Recorded Music*, 99 Music, 2000. The earliest recording of this song, this version has a rich, orchestral feel that was appropriate to the dramatic placement of the song in a romantic film.

- Frank Sinatra's languid 1949 ballad as found on *The Essential Frank Sinatra: The Columbia Years*, Columbia, 2010.
- Doris Day's plaintive delivery as found on *Golden Girl (The Columbia Recordings 1944–1966)*, Columbia, 1999.
- The most famous version of the song is the Flamingos' doo-wop version, which peaked at number eleven on the Billboard Hot 100 in 1959. As you can hear, the Flamingos play the song with a very different harmonic structure to create a spacey, almost dreamy ambience that sounds much more modern than the previous versions. As recorded by the Flamingos on *Flamingo Serenade*, Marathon, 2011.
- Ella Fitzgerald's upbeat 1962 swing version, as recorded on *Ella Swings Brightly With Nelson*, Essential Jazz Classics, 2012.
- Peter Cox and Niki Haris performed a rhythm and blues, synth-heavy version for the movie *Corrina, Corrina* in 1994. It appears on *Corrina, Corrina (Original Soundtrack)*, RCA, 1994.

As you listen to these different versions, think about which you like best and why. Which version resonates with you the most?

JAZZ PERFORMANCES OF THE GREAT AMERICAN SONGBOOK

Most Great American Songbook songs were written for a theatrical or cinematic setting. As you have learned from previous chapters, jazz singers tend to have a very different style than the singers who originally sang these songs, singers that most likely had big, formally trained voices that were able to be heard, unamplified, in large theaters. This is still true of opera singers and many Broadway singers today. However, as jazz became more popular, many great jazz musicians recorded Great American Songbook songs, remaking them in their own style. It's very important, as you develop your jazz ears and vocal jazz technique, to listen to these great recordings of the very best jazz singers singing Great American Songbook songs. Singers such as Ella Fitzgerald, Frank Sinatra, Rosemary Clooney, Mel Tormé, Lena Horne, Blossom Dearie, Billie Holiday, Sarah Vaughn, Carmen McRae, and Nat King Cole all sang songs from the Great American Songbook each in her or his own way.

In today's commercial music, popular artists seldom sing a song recorded by another popular artist or musical contemporary in a live performance setting. Most popular artists sing their own original songs or specific songs written for the artist. The usual thirty-two-measure Great American Songbook tune and its melodic line allowed for freedom of interpretation while still staying within the jazz idiom. Here are a few song interpreters of the American Songbook.

Ella Fitzgerald

Though Ella Fitzgerald is most famous for her scat improvisation, she also shows improvisational genius with her heartfelt phrasing on her 1956 album *Ella Fitzgerald Sings the Cole Porter Songbook* (Verve, 1997).

Listen to Ella's beautiful rendition of Porter's songs, honoring the composer's melody while adding her own interpretation through her rhythmic phrasing and subtle use of word emphasis and dynamics. Pay particular attention to her rendition of "Miss Otis Regrets (She's Unable to Lunch Today)" sung with a consistent tone as she floats over the chord changes. ♪

Other listening recommendations include her albums:

- *Ella Fitzgerald Sings the Irving Berlin Songbook*, Old Style, 2013.
- *Ella Fitzgerald Sings the Johnny Mercer Songbook*, Verve, 1964.

Dinah Washington

Singer Dinah Washington adds subtle R&B embellishments and blues inflections to her performances of the Great American Songbook, such as on "All of Me" from *The Complete Dinah Washington on Mercury Vol. 4 1954–1956* (Verve, 1992), as well as on "But Not for Me," as found on *The Swingin' Miss "D."* (Hallmark, 2011). ♪

Frank Sinatra

- *Frank Sinatra Sings His Greatest Hits*, Columbia/Legacy, 1997.
- *Sinatra/Jobim: The Complete Reprise Recordings*, Signature Sinatra, 2010.

- *Frank Sinatra Sings Rodgers & Hammerstein*, Columbia/Legacy, 1996.

Anita O'Day

- *Anita Sings for Oscar*, Original Jazz Sound, 2011.
- *Anita O'Day Swings Cole Porter with Billy May*, VCR Records, 2012.

Mel Tormé

- *The Great American Songbook: Live at Michael's Pub*, Telarc, 2009.
- *The Duke Ellington and Count Basie Songbooks*, Verve/Polygram/ Universal Classics & Jazz, 2005.

Carmen McRae

- *Carmen McRae Sings Great American Songwriters*, IMS, 1999.
- *The Great American Songbook*, Atlantic, 2005.

THE GREAT AMERICAN SONGBOOK AND YOU

Fake Books

Fake books began as a way for musicians to have a collection of songs with chord changes and notation for learning and playing in live performance. Around the 1950s, songs were collected and bound together in book form. However, the songs were illegally printed with no royalties paid to the composer! It was an unwritten word of mouth, from musician to musician, as to where to obtain these books. For years professional jazz musicians would purchase fake books through underground back channels, though fake books were the bible of jazz musicians. As a musician and singer myself, I was among the many who needed these fake books, though illegal at the time. I still remember the instructions from my colleague to "Look for the man on the corner with the dog. He only takes cash!" Fortunately, jazz fake books are now legal and are an incredible resource for singers.

Fake book collections are written in particular keys. However, these songs are very often transposed into another key to suit the instrument or the vocalist. So when you first look into a fake book, you will see the song written in a key that may or may not work for you.

Finding Your Song Key

Have you ever heard a song playing on the radio or your iPod, and when you start to sing along, you find you can't sing all of the notes or you hurt your throat trying to sing like the artist of the recording? That means that it's not in the right key for your voice. Finding the right song key is important so that you can sing the melody in your own natural voice without straining. When a composer writes a song, he or she will choose a specific key to write it in, but each singer who chooses to perform a song may sing the song in a different key that suits the individual singer. Below are the typical ranges for the soprano, alto, tenor, baritone, and bass voice.

To find your range, use a piano or keyboard. Start from the lowest note you can sing comfortably and slide your voice up to the highest

Typical Vocal Ranges

Figure 6.1. Typical Vocal Ranges

note you can sing comfortably. This is your vocal range. This exercise also helps warms up your voice and coordinates your breath and voice together. Sing each note smoothly even if your voice sounds light. Do not try to push the sound out! Make sure that you take a deep, low breath with each phrase you sing. Once you learn your range, you can look at what's printed in a fake book and evaluate how the song needs to be transposed for you. This is important information for you to know for yourself as well as any other musicians you may be playing with.

Which Songs Should I Learn?

There is a simple answer: whichever songs you like and "speak" to you. It is impossible to create a list of recommended songs here in the book. It is helpful, however, to construct a set list with a mix of jazz ballads, medium swing and fast swing tempos, and songs that will work with a bossa nova beat. Every singer has his or her own unique preferences and repertoire. One of the signature characteristics of a jazz singer is to have a set list that you can really own—your interpretations of these songs will become your personal Great American Songbook! Overall, the important thing is to enjoy your explorations of these great songs, and enjoy the process of learning them!

7

SCAT AND INTERPRETATION

Jazz music is rooted in improvisation. To improvise means to make up something on the spot—to create something that is not rehearsed, that is spontaneous. From the very beginning, jazz has always been "ear" music rather than written. Songs were not learned from notated music but were passed down from one musical person to another through singing, playing, and listening. Singers and players would gather. One person would begin a song and someone else might join in, adding a different melody or rhythm. The music would be instinctive but not planned. Traditionally, the chords in jazz compositions do not usually have set voicings that are written out. Occasionally, specific arrangements include notated chord voicings, but historically jazz instrumentalists have always had the prerogative to voice chord changes according to what they instinctively hear. For the singer, hearing unfamiliar jazz chord voicings on a familiar jazz standard can be a challenge. Part of being a successful jazz singer is having the skill and flexibility to respond to different chord voicings and improvise within them.

Jazz improvisation can mean many things to singers. To some it is simply scat singing. To others it is making up a new melody on a familiar song, changing the rhythmic phrasing within a melody, or adjusting the timbre of one's voice to create new textures. Often, it is a combination of all of these elements. In today's world this can become confusing to young singers aiming to sing in any style. In previous chapters, we discussed how improvisation encompasses phrasing as well as altering the melody with or without words. Not every jazz singer needs to become a master at scat. However, it is an important element of expression for the jazz singer.

You have almost certainly been in a small group singing "Happy Birthday" to someone. If you are a singer, you have probably noticed that some of the group is not really singing the correct melody even though the words of the song are correct. Jazz standards are not as familiar as the song "Happy Birthday." However, when it comes to jazz singing, if you really don't know the melody first, the jazz players accompanying you on the song—as well as the audience—will think you do not know the song at all! In the last chapter, we learned about the Great American Songbook. These standard songs are a large part of the jazz repertoire. Before attempting improvisation or melodic alterations, it is very important to establish that you know the original melody and chord progressions as written by the composer. Once you are sure of the melody, you can explore the art of melodic and rhythmic improvisation.

Typically, jazz audiences are familiar with jazz standards but may not always identify with vocal scat improvisation. Audiences expect that jazz instrumentalists will solo over a jazz song, but often don't have similar expectations of singers. For a jazz vocalist, improvisation and scat is more than just singing a jazz song and using scat syllables in the second chorus. To scat well is to learn how to listen in a different way. Jazz improvisation means altering the original melody's rhythmic notation or altering the original melody line—or both simultaneously! Listening to the great jazz artists, both vocalists and instrumentalists, will help you understand the skill of improvisation we call scat. One big difference between the singer and instrumentalists improvising is the instrumentalists have something to press—a key on the piano, a string on a guitar, a horn valve. Singers have to essentially hear and sing an improvised solo with no buttons to push, relying only on their breath and vocal technique. When you listen to Ella Fitzgerald, Sarah Vaughan, or Mel Tormé scat, it sounds so easy—until you try it!

Good overall technique and breath management are of course essential for a jazz singer. Even if you have many great improvisational and musical ideas that you think will go with a jazz standard, you still need to make sure that your intonation is accurate and that you have the vocal facility to not only sing fast passages but also to hold on to some notes. Without good technical skill, a jazz singer would not have the vocal agility and freedom to execute improvisational ideas. If your breath is not mastered, then there is a chance that your intonation will be effected. No matter how quickly you sing or how many notes you use to improvise, underneath your solo your voice should be a free-sounding tone with good intonation.

Acquiring improvisational skills is a process and very individualistic. Jazz singers utilize rhythmic phrasing, scatting, and improvising melodically while singing the lyrics. You may find improvising with the rhythmic phrasing easier or you may find it easier to focus on scat singing. A fast-improvised solo will require you to approach fast notes with fine-tuned articulation of syllables while connecting note to note as in a spoken phrase. As a beginning improviser, you may wish to choose a jazz standard in a medium tempo or easy swing groove before attempting any fast songs.

SCAT GUIDELINES

Try listening to Billie Holiday's version of "I Cover the Waterfront" or Carmen McRae's "This Will Make You Laugh." You can sing along with the artist while tapping your foot on the downbeat of the song. The second time you play the song, use your hand or foot to tap out the beats within a measure. In a song in 4/4 time, you would be tapping 1, 2, 3, 4. Listen to the solo singer and her phrasing. Is the singer coming on the first beat or slightly after? If you compare the written sheet music or a lead sheet with written melody, you will see the difference. The rhythm of the written melody can vary from player to player, singer to singer. The melody line can be embellished or altered. In the early days of blues and jazz, the majority of instrumentalists and vocalists did not read music. The written versions often came after various artists had already performed the songs for many years, and melodies were standardized in notation. ♪

Starting with well-known songs passed on from one person to another, jazz musicians would use the framework of a song and then embellish the melody according to how they felt about the music. We can hear this in Louis Armstrong's trumpet and cornet playing. We can also hear this with blues singers using speech-like inflections as a form of expression and interpretation. Horn solos could play the melody of a song but also interject slight embellishments, grace notes, and blue notes, adding to the existing melody. Blues, jazz, and rhythm and blues singers can embellish the melody in the same way, adding a growl or guttural sound. The special part of jazz improvisation is that it all needs to make musical sense with the original composition. The improvised musical phrases fit with the chord progressions of the song. The prerequisite for improvisation and scatting is good ears. You can make up your own improvised melody to a jazz standard as part of your scat solo, but unless you really hear and know the chord progression of a song, there is a good chance your improvised melody will not coincide with the chord changes. Scatting effortlessly though a song chorus takes time, listening, and practice.

There are some jazz artists who take musical chances regarding improvisation. This essentially began with the bebop era and continues today. Artists like Eddie Jefferson, King Pleasure, and Annie Ross sang instrumental solos with lyrics. Singer Betty Carter sang phrases like a horn player, bending notes and approaching particular notes with different vocal tone colors. By midcareer, Carter developed a seamless way of scatting and singing lyrics and often did not sing the actual melody of the song. She incorporated melismas, singing a song with a very slow tempo or very fast! As we have discussed in earlier chapters, some instrumentalists create new songs from jazz standards with their improvised solo. Young vocalists or aspiring jazz vocalists may hear a rendition of a song performed by a jazz fusion artist that may make such a departure from the original melody that the song really does sound new.

GUIDELINES AND EXERCISES FOR SCAT

There are many ideas and methods for teaching scat. Learning to scat easily and effortlessly takes time. Much of learning scat depends upon the orientation of the singer. For example, if you have listened to jazz for years or you play an instrument, this will likely speed up your progress, as opposed to someone very new to jazz or who does not play an

instrument. As with every aspect of learning how to sing jazz, scat singing starts with listening, listening, and more listening. The exercises
below will give you a framework to inform your listening, and give you
some concrete exercises to start building your improvisational and scat
singing skills.

The Blues Scale

Start by singing the blues scale in every key that fits within your
vocal range. Then, using either a Music Minus One twelve-bar blues
accompaniment or an existing blues jam (you can easily find these on
YouTube), sing the appropriate blues scale over the twelve bars being
played. When the band returns to the beginning, try singing only one or
two notes from the blues scale per measure.

After you do this several times, try adding three notes from the blues
scale, then four.

This exercise will help you internalize the blues scale and move easily
from note to note in different sequences. As you continue to play within
this exercise, pay attention to how you develop ease within the blues
scale and how you can start hearing ahead to what you want to sing next.

ONE/TWO NOTE BLUES SCALE EXERCISE   SHAPIRO

Figure 7.1a.   One- or Two-Note Blues Scale Exercise

3 AND 4 NOTE BLUES SCALE EXERCISE

SHAPRIO

Figure 7.1b. Three- or Four-Note Blues Scale Exercise ♪

Using Motifs

Motifs in jazz are melodic phrases that are repeated throughout the course of a solo as a whole. We can listen to instrumental motifs to help us with phrasing and how to approach scat singing, or we can write our own motif emulating the phrasing and tone color of an instrumentalist. Motifs generate cohesiveness from solo to solo throughout a song through repetition. It gives the song a hook for listeners and players to keep returning to.

Listen to the following recordings for the motifs in each solo. Pay attention to the instrumental phrasing and scat syllables and how the motifs are used to connect different solos to one another and create connections throughout the songs:

- "Now's the Time," as recorded by Charlie Parker, *20th Century Masters—The Millennium Collection: The Best of Charlie Parker*, Hip-O, 2004.
- Annie Ross of Lambert, Hendricks, and Ross came out with a solo album recorded in 1956. Her rendition of "Tain't What You Do" has a repeated motif with slight modification as she sings the words "tain't what you do." Although she sings lyrics, the style in which she sings them is easily transferable to scat. Jot down a few scat syllables to sing the phrases instead of the lyrics. Melvin "Sy" Oliver and James "Trummy" Young, "Tain't What You Do" (1939), as recorded by Annie Ross, *Annie By Candlelight*, Smith & Co., 2011 [Track 5].

- The following recording is an instrumental but later was set to words by Jon Hendricks. Listen to the original recording first. J. Giuffre, "Four Brothers" (1947), *The Thundering Herds 1945–1947 by Woody Herman*, Definitive Records, 2008. As recorded in 1977 by Manhattan Transfer, *Pastiche*, Atlantic & Atco Remasters/Rhino, 1994. You can find the lyrics in *The New Real Book 1: Jazz Classics, Choice Standards, Pop Fusion*, Sher Music Co., 1988. ♪

Playing with Rhythm

Rhythmic phrasing can serve as a guide when you begin to improvise melodically. Even if you hear the notes you want to scat, the phrasing of your improvisation is just as important as the correct notes.

Count aloud one through four as in a bar of four beats. Maintain the same tempo either by patting the four beats with your foot or with your hand patting your thigh. Then speak aloud, "Hi, how are you?" Stop for a moment tapping out the rhythm. Pretend you are saying hello to someone you have not seen in awhile and you are very glad to see your longtime friend. Say the same phrase, "Hi, how are you?" as in a conversation.

Go back to tapping four beats per measure with your foot or leg. Keep the tempo consistent. Then speak the same phrase, "Hi, how are you?" Do not try to keep the tempo you are tapping out. Instead speak the phrase aloud the same way you spoke it without any beat. Remember to put expression in speaking the phrase.

RHYTHMIC SPEAKING EXERCISE SHAPIRO

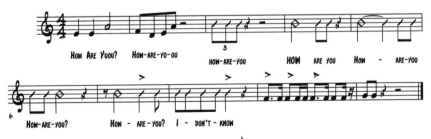

Figure 7.2. Rhythmic Speaking Exercise ♪

When we speak, we vary our rhythm; sometimes we pause, and we may get excited and talk fast. We make inflections as we speak as well as slightly emphasizing or accenting a portion of a word, a complete word, or a phrase. We do this to add expression and color to our speech, to make ourselves and our intentions more easily understood, and to communicate meaningfully with others. Communicating meaningfully in your singing is just as important and can be achieved with the same rhythmic tools that we employ effortlessly in everyday conversation.

Another exercise that can help you achieve this is to learn the melody of a jazz standard. Begin with a ballad and speak the lyrics aloud as you would a conversation. Practice this throughout the whole song first. Then sing the melody—but sing the phrases with the rhythmic phrasing you used while speaking them. This can be difficult but keep experimenting! You will start to feel a difference. Here are some examples of how every day conversational inflections enhance jazz vocals:

- Listen to Abbey Lincoln sing the lyrics "There's a sun up in the sky. Can you dig it? Can you dig it? There's more ways than one of fly. Can you dig it? Can you dig it?" in the song "Can You Dig It?" A. Lincoln and D. Wooldridge, "Can You Dig It?" (2002), as recorded by Abbey Lincoln, *It's Me*, Verve, 2003 [Track 11].
- A. Ross and W. Gray, "Twisted" (1952), as recorded by Annie Ross, *Annie Ross Twisted*, Jasmine Records, 2008 [Track 5].
- C. Petrillo, M. Samuels, and S. Nelson, "Jim" (1941), as recorded by Billie Holiday, *The Quintessential Billie Holiday Volume 9 (1940–1942)*, Sony Entertainment, 1991 [Track 11].
- Although singer-pianist Blossom Dearie weaved in and out of jazz and cabaret, her recordings below exemplify the conversational delivery and vocal inflections used by jazz singers. F. Rose and W. Hirsch, "Deed I Do" (1926), as recorded by Blossom Dearie, *Blossom Dearie*, Verve Music Group, 1989 [Track 1]. On the same CD, also listen to Blossom Dearie's recording of "Blossom's Blues."
- You can hear vocal inflections in Frank Sinatra's 1955 versions of the song "Can't We Be Friends" written by Paul James and Kay Swift in 1929. Often this song has been recorded as a swing tempo, an easy swing to a fast swing tempo. However, the 1955 interpretation by Frank Sinatra is different. Sinatra sings the little-known verse

of the song rubato. When he begins the actual song, the tempo is a slow swing ballad. Still, Sinatra relaxes his phrasing and you can hear his conversational delivery complete with vocal inflections. As you listen closely through the end of this recording, it is as if Sinatra was speaking the lyrics he sings. In one section of the song, Sinatra pauses as he sings the lyrics "and wonder why." The tempo begins again, but the swing feel is softened and the tempo is slightly slower as Sinatra ritards the last few phrases. P. James and K. Swift, "Can't We Be Friends" (1929), as recorded by Frank Sinatra, *In the Wee Small Hours of the Evening*, Capitol Records, 1998. ♪

Tone Colors and Vocal Inflections

Jazz singing allows the vocalist to interpret the song in many ways. This includes changing the tone of our voice and also subtle use of word inflections. We can identify word inflections in artists like Billie Holiday and tone colors in artists such as Sarah Vaughan. Here are examples of Sarah Vaughan utilizing tone colors as part of her song interpretation:

- G. Shearing, "Lullaby of Birdland" (1952), as recorded by Sarah Vaughan, *Sarah Vaughan and Clifford Brown*, Polygram, 2004 [Track 1].
- J. Dorsey, "I'm Glad There Is You" (1941), as recorded by Sarah Vaughan, *Sarah Vaughan and Clifford Brown*, Emarcy, 2012 [Track 7]. Sarah begins with singing the verse to the song accompanied by piano. She sings this verse freely rather than in strict time. Toward the end of the verse, you will hear Sarah Vaughan sing the phrase, "and all in—this world." On the word "in," she accents the word with quick melodic embellishments, slowing down on the word "in" before sliding down like a horn directly into the beginning of the song, "in-this-world." On the first phrase of the song, singing "of ordinary people," Sarah uses a subtle accent on the "or" of the word "ordinary."
- Listen to Sarah Vaughan's live recording of "Sassy's Blues." Q. Jones and S. Vaughan, "Sassy's Blues" (1963), as recorded by Sarah Vaughan, *Sassy Swings the Tivoli*, Verve Music Group, 1987 [Track 8]. Like a horn player, Vaughan weaves in and out of her scat solo, darkening or lightening her vocal tone for emphasis on a specific word or phrase. ♪

Watch this video clip of Nancy Wilson singing "I Thought About You": www.drummerworld.com/Videos/edthigpennancywilson.html, or www.youtube.com/watch?v=YHg8QeZwc70. This was a live concert in Germany in 1987 with jazz greats Hank Jones on piano, Eddie Gomez on bass, and Ed Thigpen on drums. Nancy sings the lyrics, "I took a trip on a train, and I thought about you." But when Nancy sings the next phrase, "I passed a shadowy lane," she bends the word/note "lane," slightly coloring her tone. When she sings, "At every stop that we made, I thought about you," Nancy varies the rhythmic phrasing, pressing slightly on the word "you" for emphasis. When she sings, "and what did I do," she slightly darkens her tone, and she sings "and what" while also bending the note/word on the same section. On the second chorus, Nancy improvises rhythmically, bending and coloring her tone. She sings, "I-took-a-trip on a train," changing her tone on the word "train," elongating the word with added embellishment. Later during her solo chorus, she bends the words on "with the same old dream," coloring her vocal tone slightly on part of this phrase. ♪

For a visual comparison, look at the original sheet music or lead sheet of this song written by Mercer and VanHeusen and then to the figure listed below. You can find this song in lead sheet form with melody and chords in the *Real Vocal Book, Volume I* published by Hal Leonard Corporation or the Sher Music publications of *The New Real Book*. Original sheet music editions can be found on many websites such as onlinesheetmusic.com. Below is Nancy Wilson's interpretation of "I Thought About You."

Figure 7.3. Nancy Wilson's Interpretation of "I Thought About You." *D. Schachter*

Compare this live recording from 1987 of "Guess Who I Saw Today" at www.youtube.com/watch?v=0DFhz_tE7EEg. If you listen carefully through this video, you will hear how Nancy Wilson bends the notes and brightens or darkens her tone in a subtle way, with subtle use of dynamics and accents as she sings the lyrics. ♪

Jazz singer Rhiannon utilizes tone color and inflections and sometimes borrows an instrumental solo as part of her scat before adding her own improvisation. On her CD *In My Prime*, listen to her recording of "So Many Stars" (S. Mendes and A. and M. Bergman "So Many Stars" [1966], as recorded by Rhiannon, *In My Prime*, Rhiannonmusic, 2005 [Track 8]). Listen to Rhiannon as she sings the phrase "which dream of all the dreams." Her vocal tone changes into more of low middle tone on the word "dream," adding to her interpretation and painting a picture of the word "dream" as if in a faraway, unapproachable place. Then listen to when she follows with "when there's a dream for every star," brightening up the word "star." ♪

For practice and review, see figure 7.4a for an exercise that will help you hear chord progressions more clearly. Learning to actually hear jazz chords is a process you will need to practice if you do not have any prior experience listening to jazz. If you play an instrument such as piano or guitar, it will help speed up your progress. One of the exercises I use with my students is singing the chords in root position, first inversion, and second inversion. You begin by singing dominant sevenths.

DOMINANT CHORDS

Figure 7.4a. Dominant Chords ♪

DOMINANT EXERICSE

CONTINUE THE SAME PATTERN ON ALL DOMINANT CHORDS

Figure 7.4b. Dominant Chord Exercise ♪

Outline the chords as in figures 7.4a and b. Sing the dominant chords up the scale and back down (figure 7.4c). Then proceed on to major seventh chords, minor chords, and diminished chords.

Once you feel like you can sing the notes within each chord at a consistent tempo, you can try singing ninth chords and so on.

DOMINANT CHORDS, ROOT AND INVERSIONS, EXTENSIONS SHAPIRO

Figure 7.4c. Dominant Chords, Roots, and Inversions ♪

Ninth Chords

Figure 7.5a. Adding Ninth Chords ♪

Aural Transcriptions

If you are a beginner, listen to "Everything Happens to Me" as recorded by Chet Baker. ♪

Learn the Chet Baker solo with the exact pitches and the rhythm he sings in his improvisational vocal solo. If you are an advanced jazz singer, listen to "Oh, Lady Be Good" as recorded by Ella Fitzgerald in 1959.

As noted above, learn Ella's scat solo with the exact pitches and rhythms she uses. Try to grasp the syllables these singers use in their solos. Pay

Major 7ths, Minor and Diminished Chord Examples

Figure 7.5b. Major Seventh Chords, Minor Chords, and Diminished Chords ♪

close attention to not only the phrasing but also the vocal inflections. At first this may sound very easy, but to sing an aural transcription exactly as the artist performs it is usually more difficult than you think.

What Syllables Do I Sing?

Scat syllables run the gamut and are very individualized by the jazz singer. Some vocalists use syllables that give the singer a certain sound. For example, you might think of your vocal solo as a trumpet player and choose syllables that would help you emulate the approach of a trumpet player, or the jazz singer could imagine her or his voice as sounding more like a saxophone or trombone.

Using scat syllables in jazz singing is a lesson in vocal articulation. Start out with one pattern that feels right for you or that you have heard from jazz greats such Ella Fitzgerald, Sarah Vaughan, Mel Tormé, Mark Murphy, Anita O'Day, or Sheila Jordan, just to name a few. You can also refer back to early jazz, listening to Louis Armstrong's trumpet and cornet playing as well as his singing and scat. Listen to the recording of Louis Armstrong playing and then singing "I Cover the Waterfront" in 1933. Another singer who also played several instruments was Leo Watson. Mostly obscure, fortunately we are able to hear Watson's scat performances on a few recordings from 1937 to 1947.

Practice speaking these syllables, but use your lips and tongue more than you think necessary! Choose one syllable at a time. Speak in an easy swing tempo. First, use the tempo of four to a measure.

You can also listen to Ella Fitzgerald and use some of her scat syllables.

Du-bah-du-bah, du-bah, du-bah
Bee-de
Bee-di-dah
Bweet-bwee-dah
Scew-e-do-do
Du-du-buh
Bah-bah bah-dah

Let's try other rhythmic combinations:

SCAT SYLLABLES EXERCISE

Figure 7.6. Scat Syllables Exercise

Scat Patterns Over Chord Progressions

Scat and phrasing listening examples (note that you can listen to any versions of these songs that you find; especially good performances available on YouTube are noted where applicable):

- Louis Armstrong, "I Cover The Waterfront," www.youtube.com/watch?v=UZvqvNYJmC4 (live in Copenhagen, 1934)
- Bing Crosby with the Rhythm Boys and early solo work, "Wa-Da-Da"
- Leo Watson, "Sonny Boy"
- Connie Boswell and Boswell Sisters, "If It Ain't Love"
- Mills Brothers, "Dinah"
- Cab Calloway, "The Scat Song"
- Sarah Vaughan, "Scat Blues," www.youtube.com/watch?v=lnh5Tyx2hT8&feature=kp (live in Berlin, 1969)
- "Shulie A Bop" from the CD set *Divine: The Jazz Albums 1954–58*, Verve, 2013
- Mel Tormé, "Hi-Fly"
- Jon Hendricks, "Shouter"
- Sheila Jordan, "Anthropology"
- Chet Baker, "You Go to My Head"
- James Moody, "Fly Me to the Moon" ♪

TRIPLET RHYTHM SCAT EXERCISE

BA-DAH-DAH-BA-DAH-DAH-BA-DAH-DAH BA-DAH DAH   DO-DEE-DEE-DO-DEE DE DO-DEE-DEE BO-DO-DEE

BU - DEE - DAH - BU - DEE - DAH - BU - DEE - DAH   BU - DEE - DAH

Figure 7.7a. Triplets Rhythmic Exercise

DOTTED EIGHTH NOTE PATTERN

BA - BA-BA - BA-BA - BA-BA - BA   DU - BA-DU - BA-DU - BA-DU - BA   DU - BA-DU - BA-DU - BA-DU - BA

Figure 7.7b. Eighth Note Rhythmic Exercise

SIXTEENTH NOTE PATTERN

DU-DA-DA-DA-DU-DA-DA-DA DU-DU-DEE-DEE-DU-DE-DU-DE   DU-DA-DU-DEE-DU-DA-DU-DEE-DU-DU-DU-DU-DEE-DU-BA

Figure 7.7c. Sixteenth Note Rhythmic Exercise

SUMMARY

Step 1. Know the correct melody and the chord progressions of the song.

Step 2. Refer to the jazz greats—vocalists and instrumentalists that have recorded the song.

Step 3. Practice singing the song in various tempos.

Step 4. Try singing the rhythm and some of the notes that the bassist is playing.

Step 5. Listen intently to the drum player. Choose one of the rhythmic patterns that the drummer is playing and try to emulate the same sound and rhythm throughout the whole song.

Step 6. Sing the song as written with the chord progressions being played either by a pianist or guitarist or Music Minus One track.

Step 7. Sing the melody without words. You can try using some scat syllables.

Step 8. Sing the melody again, but alter a few notes, always referring back to the melody.

Of course you can make changes to the above list; there is no set order in the way you should practice these skills. Just let your imagination run free and your voice will follow. As you gain confidence in your vocal technique, articulation, and melodic understanding, your soloing and improvisation will start coming more naturally.

8

JAZZ VOCAL PERFORMANCE

There are many elements of successful contemporary vocal jazz performance, including a high level of musicianship, a working knowledge of microphones and PA systems, and an ability to communicate clearly with other musicians, regardless of the ensemble setup. While today it is important and expected that jazz musicians can read music and speak comfortably about notation and key signature, historically, jazz vocalists and instrumentalists did not read music. However, taking a cue from classical musicians to achieve creditability, early jazz instrumentalists began to learn notation, especially during the big band era, when complicated arrangements became the norm. Reading notes on the page was not considered as important as the musicians' ear for music. As time went on, reading music, particularly for instrumentalists, became a more standard skill.

In the early years female vocalists who sang blues and jazz in the 1930s were not expected to read music and did not have any opportunities to learn. Since blues and jazz were not formally taught in America, this skill was considered improper for young women, so there wasn't any structured system of learning the music. Instead of knowing music theory or how to read notation, these early singers were expected to know a collection of songs and be able to carry a tune.

Vocalists often didn't know his or her song key of a familiar jazz standard. Often a pianist or guitarist would have to teach the vocalist a new song or the singer would listen to the song on a recording. Even the most famous of jazz singers have had this problem, as demonstrated in a brief film clip of a 1955 rehearsal in Los Angeles with Billie Holiday. Her pianist asks, "What key do you do it in?" Billie chuckles and replies, "I don't know. What key do I do it in?" (https://www.youtube.com/watch?v=E9Dr-iU5Dw0). The pianist had to guess what song key would work as Billie began singing, "Please Don't Talk About Me When I'm Gone." Frequently bandleaders coddled famous singers of the 1940s and 1950s. Band members had no expectations of the singer except to look nice, stand up tall, and sing into the microphone. It was assumed that the natural musicality of the jazz vocalist, vocal tone, and interpretation would just be there. These factors were more important that knowing musical notation and song keys. Many of the jazz singers of the 1940s through the 1960s did not even count off the song. It was one of the accompanying musicians or the bandleader that would count the tempo.

Remember that during this time period, women were not really considered equal to men. For male musicians, it was a duel-edged sword. On one hand, male musicians wanted the vocalist to be musically responsible. On the other hand, the American culture in the 1940s through the 1950s was that the women were subservient to men. Still there was an underlying resentment of singers by the instrumentalists that tirelessly practiced their instruments daily while the singer appeared to barely practice other than to memorize songs. The singer stood in front of the band and enjoyed the applause and acclaim while the instrumentalists sat behind the singer and played. The backing musicians, except for the bandleader, usually did not receive much recognition. Sometimes a vocalist's appearance even took precedent over the vocal tone and delivery, rendering the actual music completely unnoticed. In listening to the more notable big band singers and some lesser-known bands, you can find novelty songs that were usually upbeat and not necessarily composed for their musicality. For example, listen to big band singer Nancy Norman with the Sammy Kaye band on the recording "Chickery Chick." You can find this recording on collections recorded by the Sammy Kaye band on iTunes and YouTube and on the CD *Swing and Sway with Sammy Kaye: 21 of His Greatest Hits.* ♪

The stigma of an uneducated jazz vocalist who knows nothing about music theory and musicianship is still out there. However musically ignorant even the most talented singers of yesteryear were, today's jazz singers are expected to be knowledgeable musicians in their own right. While in the past, a vocalist would not even know his or her song key; modern jazz singers should take care to learn at least rudimentary music theory and develop musicianship skills. Aspiring jazz vocalists of the present day usually study voice, just as an instrumentalist would study their instrument in order to play with good technique. This can involve voice lessons, a vocal coach, and intense study on vocal technique, as well as learning song keys, improvisation, music notation, and how to write lead sheets.

MICROPHONES

In the early years of jazz, there were not many choices regarding microphones or sound systems. Early blues singers traveling in tent shows or carnivals did not have microphones. Instead, they projected their voices over whatever ambient noise existed during their performance. By the 1930s, microphones were more commonly used. One of the early microphones used by blues and jazz vocalists, called a ribbon microphone, was developed by RCA in 1931 and is pictured in figure 8.1.

Vocalists did not carry a microphone with them. They sang through a house PA system and whatever microphone the venue offered. With no choice about amplification, vocalists had no power over what they sounded like to the audience. The microphone likely did not have the capacity to carry a specific timbre of a vocalist, and either the venue staff or perhaps one of the musicians controlled the volume setting. Musicians were often standing or sitting, playing behind the singer, so it could be difficult to tell what the actual sound of the vocalist was in a large band or big band setting.

Luckily today there are many types of microphones that provide a lot more control over your sound. Some microphones are best suited for the recording studio, some for live performance, and some for both. Choosing a microphone can be overwhelming because there are many types

Figure 8.1. Early RCA Ribbon Microphone. Used by permission from Coutant.org

of microphones and many companies that are making them! There is an array of vocal microphones with varying characteristics and prices available. If you have not used a microphone before, it can be even more confusing. The tried and true microphone companies include Shure, Beyerdynamic, AKG, Sennheiser, Neumann, and Electro-Voice. Looking at these companies is a good way to start in your search for a vocal microphone. Since there is a large selection of microphones available to you, it is best to do some research ahead of time.

When you go to a music store to purchase a microphone, you need to understand how the microphone works. Remember, as a jazz singer, the microphone will be bringing your voice out to the audience. When you watch a vocal jazz performance, notice what microphones the vocalist is using. Have an idea of what kind of brands of microphone you are considering before going into the store, as well as what kind of situations for which you will be using it. This will help a salesperson guide you in the right direction. However, it's important to work with someone knowledgeable about specific vocal microphone characteristics.

There are several types of microphones used for live vocal performance, primarily differentiated by their directionality or polar pattern, which indicates how sensitive the microphone is to sound at different angles relative to its center. From a live vocal jazz performance perspective, a unidirectional microphone is best. This kind of microphone will pick up sound from only one direction. The three subcategories of uni-directional microphones are cardioid, supercardioid, and hypercardioid. Each of these picks up sound slightly differently. Cardioid microphones pick up sound from the front and sides of the microphone and reject most sounds from the rear of the microphone, while supercardioid and hypercardioid pick up a more focused sound from the front of the mi-crophone and less from the sides of the microphone and are thus more strongly directional than cardioid mics. These microphones pick up some sound from the rear of the microphone as well. The differences between these three polar patterns are subtle, and your preference for any one will depend on your individual voice and performance style. Try out microphones with varying polar patterns to see what works best with your voice.

Microphones also differ in construction. While there are many types of microphones, the main choices for live vocal performance

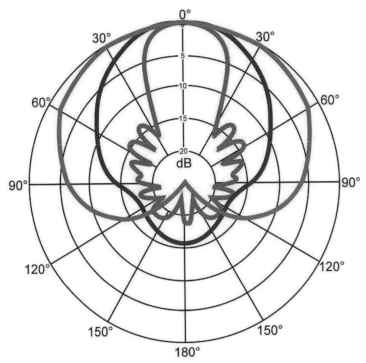

Figure 8.2. Polar Patterns of Microphones. *Soundonsound.com/ Google Free Images*

are dynamic microphones and condenser microphones. Dynamic microphones, by far the most economical and common choice for live performance, have a thin diaphragm within that moves in response to sound and creates an electrical current, resulting in amplification. Dynamic microphones are generally fairly sturdy, which is a plus for live gigs, and can handle high decibel levels. They do not require external power to operate. While dynamic microphones tend to pick up less vocal nuance than other kinds of microphones, they are a good choice for your first microphone.

Condenser microphones, which require an external power source to operate, were more traditionally found in the recording studio than on stage. While dynamic microphones require the input sound to do the work of moving their internal diaphragm and creating a charge, condenser microphones' internal diaphragm is already charged by the external power source. Thus, the input sound (your voice) does less work on the inner mechanism of the microphone, resulting in a more nuanced output. Condenser microphones will pick up more of the variations within your tone. Many pop singers today prefer using condenser microphones. This includes wireless microphones that are condenser mics.

A third kind of microphone, the above-mentioned ribbon microphone, began to see use in live vocal performances sometime in the late 1960s with the development of the Beyer Dynamic M500 handheld ribbon microphone. It is difficult to determine the exact years, but ribbon microphones were used primarily in U.S. news broadcasts from about 1920 through 1950. Ribbon microphones are still used in the recording studio. Ribbon microphones work with a thin ribbon membrane suspended between two magnets that vibrate upon encountering sound waves. Like condenser microphones, ribbon microphones are also extremely sensitive to vocal nuance but are extremely fragile. They are also bidirectional, meaning they take in sound in a figure-eight pattern from both the front and back of the microphone. Current models for vocalists are expensive. There are some traditional jazz singers that prefer the warm and natural sound of the ribbon microphone, especially in small intimate performance settings with a trio or duo as accompaniment. You may encounter ribbon microphones in the recording studio, but a dynamic or condenser microphone is probably what you will see most in modern live performances.

In additional to polar pattern and microphone construction, another specification to pay attention to when purchasing a microphone is frequency response. A frequency response from 20 Hz to 20,000 Hz covers all the frequencies we can hear. Eighty Hz to 15,000 Hz is adequate for most instruments and vocals. I find that a microphone that has a frequency response higher than 15,000 Hz is able to pick up more of the high overtones, which can be an advantage for a jazz singer. It's all up to you and how you want your voice to be portrayed to the audience.

Proximity effect is another important aspect of microphone performance. This means that when you're singing into a unidirectional microphone, as you get closer to the microphone capsule, your voice becomes increasingly "boomy"-sounding. Singing right up on a unidirectional mic will typically yield a "bassier" tone. Different mics exhibit different proximity effects, and it's an important factor to consider. A person with a thicker voice—especially one who likes (or needs) to sing right up on the mic—will want a microphone with less proximity effect. A person with a thin voice might benefit a great deal from a microphone with more pronounced proximity effect.

Purchasing a microphone is an investment. Scrutinize your options regarding price. A good microphone will be able to bring out all of the overtones of your voice. A cheap microphone from an unknown company will not. The best way to choose a mic is to sing through it before you purchase. In some larger music stores, you will be able to try out the microphone hooked up to a PA system. This would also be a good time to check out PA systems as well! Let's assume you are at a music store with a microphone or two that you have chosen to try. The microphone is hooked up to one of the sound systems. Before you add reverb or effects to your microphone, listen to the microphone with no effects at all.

Speak into the microphone with your normal speaking voice, and then speak in higher and lower registers. Sing into the microphone and sing in different registers of your voice. Try singing softly as well as in your normal singing volume. Listen to the clarity of the sound as you sing in your low, mid, and upper registers. The microphone should sound clear in every part of your voice. If the sound is muddy in the bottom of your register or lacks natural brilliance in your upper register, then this is not the microphone for you. Look for a microphone with a wide frequency response. Remember that the microphone should not cloud or hide any aspect of your voice.

Microphones are a very complex topic. As a vocalist, it's important that you know what works for you and why. You can learn more about

Figure 8.3. Proper Microphone Position

microphone specifications and technology through many excellent online resources. Rudy Trubitt's 1997 book *Live Sound for Musicians* is now dated, as technology continues to change even more rapidly since this book first came out. But if you want a good basic overview that is easy to read, it is still an excellent resource for understanding the basics.

Microphone Stands vs. Holding the Mic

Jazz singers sing with the microphone on a microphone stand or sing holding the microphone. You will see experienced jazz singers utilize both techniques with ease. If you are new to using a microphone, the first thing to learn is where to position the microphone at your mouth. First, be sure you don't "eat" the microphone or hold it so that the mic is touching your lips! However, don't hold the microphone too far away from you either. The audience needs to hear your voice through the PA system, and as you learned above, different microphones have varying optimum distances for sound pickup at different volumes. As a jazz singer, you will get the best sound by holding the microphone at a slant (or having the microphone at a slant in the stand) while still singing into the ball of the microphone. This also allows your audience to see more of your facial expressions as you sing. With proper monitoring on stage (speakers that allow you to hear how you sound through the PA system), you will learn how to optimally use the microphone as you sing at different volumes within a song. Like everything else, microphone technique has a learning curve and is very personal. You will, with practice, become proficient.

LEAD SHEETS

For the most part, in the past, singers did not carry any music or specific lead sheets with them to a performance or rehearsal. Lead sheets, sometimes called chord sheets, notate a song in a different and shorter way than traditional sheet music. Lead sheets include the melody and lyrics, but instead of written-out piano accompaniment, there are only chord symbols notated. Sheet music editions contain the original written melody, but the notated accompaniment may sound more classical. Chord symbols on a lead sheet indicate the harmony that goes with the notated melody.

When playing in a small ensemble—a trio, quartet, quintet, or sextet—jazz musicians use lead sheets. The melody is sung by the vocalist or played by one of the musicians. The accompanying harmony is played according to the chord symbols, which lay out the chord progression. However, the voicings used by the pianist and guitarist are not written out and are up to individual musicians and the ensemble to interpret, unless there is a specific arrangement with a written-out voicing of the chords.

Figure 8.4 is an example of a sheet music edition.

Written in 1937, this song was showcased in the Broadway show entitled *Blue Devil*. Figure 8.5 shows the lead sheet version of the same song.

To be able to read and play jazz chord progressions, musicians have to learn what the chord symbols mean. For example, figures 8.6a and b are what C dominant 7, C major 7th, and C minor look like.

Jazz singers need to know a song's original melody written by the composer. You can check the original sheet music edition and compare the written melody on it to the one on the lead sheet. Remember that some jazz standards in sheet music form may not have the chord changes indicated. If there is written-out music and chord changes, you should check to see if the chord changes are correct. With older sheet music editions, there are mistakes. Even in some Fake Books or Real Book editions, there can be chord and notation mistakes, so it's important that you check notation and chords before presenting a lead sheet to your accompanist or band. You can find many jazz standards in jazz Fake Books, confusingly also called Real Books.

Although it's true that you can pay someone else to write out all of your music in lead sheet form in your song key, consider learning how to write some yourself. Reading music notation is an important element of writing lead sheets. The more proficient you are in writing lead sheets and reading music, the more effectively you will be able to communicate with other musicians.

Figure 8.4. "I See Your Face Before Me" Original Sheet Music. *Used by permission of P. Schwartz Publisher*

Figure 8.5. **"I See Your Face Before Me" Lead Sheet.** *Used by permission of P. Schwartz Publisher*

Jazz Chord Symbol Example

Figure 8.6a. **Jazz Chord Symbol Examples**

Jazz Chord Extension Examples

Root position

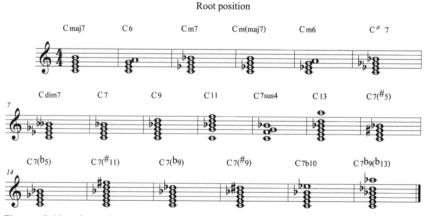

Figure 8.6b. **Jazz Chord Extensions Example**

A JAZZ SINGER'S PREPARATION

There are still old musician jokes referring to the lack of musical knowledge of jazz and pop singers. This also includes the vocalist that may not know how to plug in the microphone cord or set up the individual vocal channel on a PA system mixer. In the past, singers knew nothing about the microphone or the PA system or individual channels. Another band member would set up the microphone sound for the vocalist in the band. When you think of it, how would it be if the vocalist came over to the bassist and adjusted the sound? The bass player would not be amused. Some musicians may admire a singer's vocal skill, but the credibility and respect of jazz and pop vocalists is dependent upon several factors including professional demeanor, appropriate apparel, and preparation.

Demeanor and Timeliness

A professional singer should not have an attitude about what he or she expects from the accompanist the first time they work together. Don't show a temper or become angry if the accompanist does not play your particular arrangement quite right. And it seems like common sense, but show up to your rehearsals and gigs on time and ready to work. In other words, having a "diva-tude" is not admirable. If you are starting out as a jazz vocalist, develop a reputation as a professional vocalist who works hard and is easy to be around. Even if you have a great voice and great jazz style, if your attitude is bad and you develop a reputation as a difficult person, you won't get calls for jobs. Professional instrumentalists want to work with someone who is conscientious, responsible, and accommodating.

Apparel

If you are not sure what to wear to a particular gig, check with the accompanist or bandleader. If it is your gig, you should check out the dress code in a club or event. However, even if the audience in a club or party may be casual, think about the persona you wish to portray as a jazz singer and dress accordingly. Jazz performance has a tradition of very stylish apparel. Take a look at vintage style icons like Billie Holiday, Sammy Davis Jr., Thelonious Monk, Frank Sinatra, Nina Simone, Sarah Vaughan, and Anita O'Day. For modern inspiration, look at the Marsalis brothers, Janelle Monáe, and Esperanza Spalding. Above all, you want to feel comfortable performing in whatever you choose. If you think dressing in a dazzling, sparkly cocktail dress or a sharp Rat Pack–style suit will best suit your style and performance, go for it. If you would feel most comfortable in something a bit more subdued, that's what you should wear. There are no hard and fast rules about style for jazz performance, but in general you want to look polished and feel comfortable. Be true to your personal style while looking as good as you can. Your confidence will shine through in your performance.

Basic Preparation

At the very least, basic preparation includes the following: have your songs memorized and ready to perform in the correct keys, and have legible lead sheets for all of the musicians in the band. You should be able to count off the tempo for every song that you are performing and use professional music terms to describe tempo or arrangement of a song. Bring your own personal microphone and cord and know how to set up. Warm up by vocalizing to ensure that you are ready to sing.

LINGO FOR JAZZ SINGERS

We discussed what singing a full chorus means to most jazz musicians. Another important term is "bridge." For example, you might say, "I will sing a full chorus, you can take a solo, and I will come back in on the bridge." Another common term is "comping." This means the chordal instruments, piano or guitar, are playing the chord changes of a song without the melody. Comping occurs when instruments are playing behind a vocalist or solo instrumentalist.

What Is a Chorus?

Jazz musicians call a typical jazz standard (two verses, bridge, and back to verse) sung once through a chorus. This is a different meaning than when discussing, for example, folk songs with a "verse chorus verse" structure. A chorus in jazz really refers to the song as a whole, as described above.

Two-Beat Feel

Two-beat feel means the song may be in 4/4 meter, but the feel is 1-2, 1-2 rather than 1, 2, 3, 4. The bass would play on beats 1 and 3, sometimes alternating by playing a string on every beat, 1-2-3-4, while the drummer is accenting beats 1 and 3. In the big band era, the drummer would play the bass drum on every beat with the bassist. The guitarist would be comping with short guitar strokes on every beat. The best way to understand this is to listen to a jazz trio live or on recordings. Also listen to the bands that recorded during the big band era such as the Count Basie band.

TWO-BEAT FEEL

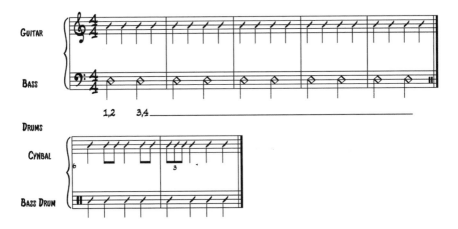

Figure 8.7. Example of Two-Beat Jazz Feel

Latin Feel or Bossa Nova

The terms Latin feel or bossa nova mean that in the A section (verses) of a song, the groove is Latin feel but can also have a swing on the bridge and for each solo. Examples of standard jazz songs that might use this format would include "Green Dolphin Street" and "Night and Day." Utilizing a Latin feel to a swing feel is dependent upon how the singer and accompanying instrumentalists interpret the song. Listen to the many versions of the above-mentioned songs to gain a better concept of how this works. Often the transition from Latin to swing, swing back to Latin is so smooth that you may have heard it in songs but did not really notice the change of rhythmic groove. The overlying tempo is the same, but the groove is different.

Head of the Tune

Head of the tune refers to the beginning of the song. You are more likely to encounter this term with older, more experienced jazz musicians, as it's a more "old-school" description.

Working with well-seasoned and experienced musicians, you may hear them say after a solo "go back to the head" instead of saying "to the beginning." I recall some performances when an instrumentalist simply nodded and said, "Head!"

Tag Ending

This term means repeating the ending of a song—usually the last two measures—three times. The common tag ending is singing the ending with lyrics, humming, or scatting the ending three times. It is often a mix of all of these things. Some recorded examples of a tag ending:

- "Squeeze Me," Jan Shapiro, *Back to Basics*, 2006.
- "I'm Gonna Sit Right Down and Write Myself a Letter," Sarah Vaughan, *The Complete Sarah Vaughan on Mercury, Vol. 3*, Mercury, 1987. ♪

Rubato or Ad-Lib

Singing ad-lib or rubato is a skill that was discussed in an earlier chapter in regard to jazz characteristics. Today we don't hear the term *ad-lib* used as much as *rubato*. Ad-lib means without restraint or limit, in accordance with one's wishes. So a singer can choose to sing a verse ad-lib, or out of tempo, usually at the beginning or ending of a song. Rubato means a fluctuation of tempo within a musical phrase. When you ask the accompanist to "ad-lib/rubato on the opening verse," the jazz singer will then have the option to phrase rhythmically free in and out of tempo, hold a word/note out longer for emphasis, run phrases together as part of interpretation using different dynamics, or some combination of all of these things. The singer can start out rubato on a verse, sing a phrase or two in a set tempo, and then return to phrasing freely. The singer can also slowly slide into a word and use contrasting dynamics. There are many options with rubato or ad-lib, and with clear communication with your band or accompanist, you will be able to express yourself freely and confidently.

WORKING WITH PIANO OR GUITAR: THE DUO

In the early days of blues, often a piano or a guitar was the only accompaniment for the vocalist. Solo blues and jazz pianists played in small clubs or events. Sometimes the singer and accompanying instrumentalist sang together. A duo is an intimate setting. The accompanying musician must provide the rhythm of the song as well as the chord changes. Generally, the accompanist voices the chords so they are complementary to the vocalist's delivery and interpretation. In a duo performance, the jazz vocalist cannot hide any vocal imperfections. When there is a trio, quartet, or larger, there are other instruments playing. The mesh of vocals with guitar or piano as well as bass and drums can sometimes divert attention to the overall band sound. In a duo, the singer can't hide.

Singing with only piano or guitar can be challenging. The tempo and the groove depend upon both the accompanist and the singer. One instrument must do the jobs of drums, bass, and chordal instruments all at the same time. Some vocalists prefer a duo to a larger band. To hear and understand the unique communication between singer and accompanist, listen carefully to these recordings:

- "You Must Believe In Spring," Bill Evans and Tony Bennett, *Tony Bennett and Bill Evans Together Again*, ToBill Entertainment Corp., 1977 [Track 5]. ♪

- "Angel Eyes," Carmen McRae [with Don Abney on piano], *The Complete Kapp Recordings Book of Ballads*, Fresh Sound Records, 2012 [Track 11].
- "You Go To My Head," Ella Fitzgerald [with guitarist Joe Pass], *Take Love Easy*, Pablo, 1991 [Track 8].
- "A Timeless Place (The Peacocks)," Tierney Sutton, *Unsung Heroes*, Telarc. 2000 [Track 3].
- "Illusion," Gregory Porter, *Water*, Motema, 2010 [Track 1]. ♪

Plan your set list beforehand, and mix up the tempos. Be ready to count off the tempo you want for the song, and decide the format. Are you singing the song once through, followed by an instrumental solo, and then back to the bridge of the song until the end? Or are you singing one chorus, then singing the second chorus as an improvised solo, followed by an instrumental solo, and then back to the chorus or the beginning of the song?

No matter which instrumentalists you are playing with, it's best to have a folder of your music in your song key with you at your gig. If it is the first time working with a specific musician, pianist or guitarist, you might want to bring a song list as well.

WORKING WITH A TRIO

The combination of jazz vocalist with accompanying trio has been a familiar performing unit for some time. In order to communicate to the trio in a professional manner, the jazz singer should be confident in counting off tempos. In a nightclub venue or simply a jazz jam, the singer needs to know how to count off the band in fast or slow swing, ballad, and bossa nova rhythms. The exception would be a vocalist and trio that have worked together for a long time. The band would then know the repertoire of the jazz singer and the usual tempos of each song. In an actual performance where the singer and trio are performing a show, the band would know the songs in each vocal set.

Experienced jazz vocalists usually have a collection of jazz standards planned for each set. The vocalist may have written lead sheets or charts or a specific written arrangement for a song. Before the set begins, the vocalist can talk through the songs particularly if there is a specific arrangement.

- When Carmen McRae sings "Time After Time" with her trio you can hear how the three instrumentalists and McRae sound as a unit. *Carmen McRae and Her Trio*, Synergie, 2013.
- Cheryl Bentyne of the Manhattan Transfer demonstrates her relaxed vocal phrasing with her swinging trio on "You'd Be So Nice To Come Home To," on *Talk of the Town*, Telarc, 2002 [Track 1].
- Mel Tormé sings "Stairway to the Stars" and "Pick Yourself Up" live with his trio on *An Evening with Mel Tormé Live From the Disney Institute*, Concord Records, 1996. ♪

PLAYING WITH A LARGE BAND OR BIG BAND

Big band singer Helen Forrest sang with Benny Goodman's band and later trumpeter Harry James's band. If you view YouTube clips of Helen Forrest's singing, you will notice that often she sings without a microphone. Keep in mind that film clips in the 1930s and 1940s during the big band era were the precursor of videos that many contemporary bands and singers use as a promotional tool today. It's unlikely that the singer in a big band would actually perform without a microphone!

Today, a vocalist performing with a sixteen-piece big band is rare. But during the 1930s and 1940s, vocalists gained almost all of their experience singing with a big band. If you have the opportunity to sing with a big band, you will need to know the songs you will be singing beforehand. The singer should ask the bandleader the tempos of each song and talk through the arrangement. This is because large bands usually have set arrangements written for the band, wherein each section of the band is required to read and know the specific arrangement. In many cases, the arrangement may not resemble the usual way you sing a particular song. You also might be asked to sing the song in a different song key.

The big bands from the 1930s and 1940s and their vocalists sounded smooth and rehearsed. If you listen to recordings from this era, you might think that it would be easy to sing with a larger band. In some cases, we don't recognize the skill of the big band vocalist with the sixteen-piece band members wailing behind. As you listen to these singers, realize the swing phrasing artistry of the vocalists and the difficulty of hearing yourself sing! Referring back to the big band era and listening to the particular arrangements can help you hear and feel the driving swing groove.

- "Everyday I Have the Blues," Joe Williams and the Count Basie Band, *Count Basie Swings–Joe Williams Sings*, Verve Music Group, 1993 [Track 1].
- Anita O'Day began her career singing with big bands. When she sings "Four Brothers," she begins by singing along with the horns with the same hornlike articulation. *Anita O'Day Sings The Winners*, Verve, 1990 [Track 6].
- Listen and watch Anita O'Day in rare film footage with the Les Brown Band at www.youtube.com/watch?v=NN3bPP42td0.
- As a young vocalist in 1939, Ella Fitzgerald sang "Jumpin' Jive" with her band at the Savoy in New York City. Written by bandleader and singer Cab Calloway, Ella's performance demonstrates her innate swing feel. Unfortunately, this particular recording is not currently available. Keep looking for it! ♪

SUMMARY

The most important element of success as a jazz vocalist is not only raw vocal talent. It is also your professionalism as a musician and a performer. Educate yourself beyond vocal technique. Learn how to prepare lead sheets and confidently discuss musical elements of your performance. Be a courteous team player with your band or accompanist. Be prepared with your song or set list. Have your own microphone and mic cord, know how to use them, and know how to hold the microphone when you sing. Understand the swing feel and how to communicate the time feel. Know the tempos and how to count off the tempo to the accompanist or band. You are a jazz singer—you are a musician!

9

JAZZ SINGING AS A CAREER

In this book, you have learned about the history and origins of jazz. You have learned about vocal jazz characteristics by listening to great performances of songs from the Great American Songbook. You have learned about scat and interpretation and how to practice these techniques to develop your own unique style and voice. You have learned about what it takes to become a good musician who can communicate with other musicians in a gig or rehearsal setting. You have learned how to listen to jazz and how to develop your jazz ears to evaluate jazz performances. Hopefully, you have learned that you must be dedicated and disciplined to develop your craft. Excellence in jazz singing is dependent on musical talent combined with a strong desire to perform and share music with others. In this book, we have essentially reviewed the history of jazz and guidelines for learning this particular style of singing. This does not mean that if you read this book, listen, and study jazz, that in a manner of months or even a year you will be the next Ella Fitzgerald, Sarah Vaughan, or Mel Tormé!

Jazz has different meanings and different applications for different singers. For some, learning to sing jazz is something you have always wanted to do because you have a passion for the music and have always loved to listen to it. For some it is an avocation, a way to share knowledge about jazz with others. For some it is a vehicle to reach students in a classroom, and for others it is a professional career. However, no matter your practical reasons for singing jazz, we all sing jazz because jazz allows us to express ourselves in a unique way through the language of the jazz idiom. We use our voice to emulate instruments, we phrase words and notes differently, we utilize conversational inflections and embellishments, we use subtle and gradual dynamics, and we improvise. We are singers who find our passion and self-expression in the singing of jazz. No other form of American music has the deep history of improvisation, interpretation, and self-expression than jazz. While it seems to outsiders that making up a song or music is easy, we know that it is not! The jazz singer needs to have a cultivated musical ear to truly perfect the art of singing jazz.

THE PASSION

In jazz or in any art, the desire to grow and develop your art is as important as being naturally gifted with vocal talent. A jazz singer's performance can evoke particular feelings and emotions not only to the singer but also to the audience. Throughout history, not all singers who became famous were the most technically perfect singers. We remember these singers because of their passion for singing and their emotional delivery of their song performance. Singers like Édith Piaf did not have the largest voice. It was her ability to infuse each of her performances with deep emotions that touched audiences and packed performance halls. Even when vocalist Judy Garland had lost much of her voice to drug and alcohol abuse, people still came to hear her sing. Her voice was broken, but she was able to still convey great feeling into her song delivery. Billie Holiday and Little Jimmy Scott reached audiences with their way of feeling a song along with their fluent improvisational abilities. For these vocalists the skill of being able to connect emotionally with the song and to the audience was exceptional. However, every jazz singer has his or her way to express the meaning of the lyric and the music. Each jazz singer has his or her own way of interpreting the music.

In the early days of blues and jazz, many great artists encountered sexism, racism, a lack of access to formal training and schooling, and many other hardships along the way. Many of them grew up in very poor and difficult circumstances. They had to struggle to perform the music they loved. There may have been some marginally easier paths for them to follow, but they were compelled to bring their music to the world. Their innate talent and desire to sing and play music was a lifelong passion and ensured career longevity.

In 1990, when I was conducting research on the influence of the Boswell Sisters and other early jazz artists, one of the many interviews I did was with blues and jazz vocalist Joe Williams. At that time, Joe Williams was seventy-one years old and still touring and performing. Sitting down with him on a break between shows, we discussed the difficulty of maintaining a career in jazz present and future. What I remember most about this amazing interview was what he said at the end of our conversation: "You sing because you have to." If you have a passion for singing jazz, you will find a way to perform. In the past chapters, we have discussed knowledge and steps to develop your jazz chops in order to sing traditional jazz. We discussed how to practice and what great artists to listen to and emulate. Where you go from here is an individual choice.

HONE YOUR CRAFT AND KEEP EXPERIMENTING

What makes some vocalists artists and others not so much? An artist is disciplined, dedicated to his or her chosen subject, and has exceptional skill. No matter how good your voice may sound and how much you love to sing, without good technique, you would be misleading yourself. Jazz vocal artistry and performance skills do not come quickly. Great jazz singers of the past had the advantage of trying out their songs nightly or at least weekly in front of many different audiences. Today, we know that finding a place to perform jazz is a challenge. Formerly, jazz singers had the opportunity to hone their skills working repeatedly with the same band. This doesn't always happen today. You must be more creative in honing your skills.

As this book has repeatedly reinforced, listen to the great jazz vocalists and instrumentalists. Listen to all the works of one particular artist to help you hear the development of the artist throughout his or her career. This development is not always obvious, but as you develop stronger listening skills, you will notice more. It really is acceptable to emulate or copy an artist's phrasing or improvisation when you are practicing. Take the time to develop note and pitch accuracy especially when learning fast instrumental passages. Eventually, learning or borrowing some of the style of a particular jazz artist will guide you on your own path of experimentation that works with your own voice.

Practicing your art involves listening to jazz, singing, and performing. Try recording yourself when you sing. Listen to how you approach the music you are singing. Listen to your phrasing. For aspiring jazz vocalists, the challenge is to know the music of the jazz standards before attempting advanced interpretation or experimentation. Study the lyrics of all the songs you learn as well as the rhythm and melody. Your interpretation and delivery of the lyrics is the true vehicle that reaches the listener, even those not usually exposed to jazz.

Another element of singing jazz is to create your own definition of success. Do you want to be able to perform locally a few times a month? Do you want to make a living as a jazz singer? Do you want to become famous? Where do you see your passion for jazz taking you?

REALITY CHECK

The most difficult thing to do as a jazz singer, or truly any kind of musician or artist, is to maintain the discipline and inspiration to continually improve your art even under disappointing circumstances. While you are trying to find performance venues so you can perform and develop your craft, you will likely have to find something else you can do during the day to cover your expenses. Supporting yourself as a musician, particularly a jazz singer, will almost certainly not be immediately possible. While you are living a double life as someone's employee during the day and a jazz singer at night, you must find the energy and discipline to come home from work at the end of the day and cultivate your jazz sound or rehearse with other musicians.

Although there has always been competition in the music world, today's advances and changes has made it even more pronounced. Modern technology has allowed us to hear music on the Internet for free or to purchase single tracks in .mp3 form. We each have our own personal playlist on our computer, tablet, and phone. The musical audience is not only within the United States but also all over the world. Popular videos stream on YouTube of nearly any genre or artist you would like to hear. Music has never been cheaper, more plentiful, or more easily accessible. While this is good for consumers and listeners, the landscape has changed for musicians who used to rely on revenue from recorded music to support themselves and continually create new recordings for their fans. Streaming applications like Pandora and Spotify play music on all of our devices. Unfortunately, this does not aide in the performers' sale of their music, even if it is very popular on these specific sites. Audiences of today tend to purchase a song they like rather than the artist—or they just stream it and do not purchase it at all. As with every era, economic conditions changed the usual musical career paths. Technology has made it easier to hear music, but CDs, for the most part, no longer sell.

Technology has changed the vehicle and mechanisms for artists to be heard. With the advent of increasing Internet-based technology, all musicians, including jazz performers, have been negatively affected. In addition to the changed sales and consumption model for musical distribution, performance spaces, particularly small and medium-sized venues, have also become less profitable. Where there were several jazz nightclubs in a medium-sized city, there may now be only one. Many local radio stations that played jazz have slimmed down their programming. Even in the case of NPR and PBS, two public organizations that continue to embrace the arts, jazz radio programs have been slowly replaced and hours of radio jazz play have been cut. Boston's own iconic PBS radio station, WGBH, faced this very situation. WGBH not only presented jazz every night but also supported local jazz artists by having live guest appearances on the radio. This gave exposure for local jazz performers that helped to cultivate an audience for live jazz. Three years ago, in July 2012, the radio manager decided to cut the nightly jazz program of *Eric in the Evening*, replacing it with talk radio. The *Eric in the Evening* radio program is now relegated to three hours a night on Friday, Saturday, and Sunday evenings. This is just one example of how listening to jazz on local radio is becoming obsolete.

The upside of changing technology is that now almost anyone can record their music on music software and promote it through the Internet. There are Internet radios stations and podcasts that will play unknown jazz artists and original compositions. Internet radio has essentially replaced local radio jazz music programing with its own varied jazz playlists. However, because music software is available to everyone anywhere, there is more competition to simply be heard. There are many Internet radio formats that can be heard all over the world. This is good for jazz artists, but there is no sure way to really establish a fan base for your music.

Jazz radio on the Internet may include artists and music that would not have been considered jazz at all even ten years ago. On an Internet jazz station, you are more likely to hear R&B/jazz fusion performers like Jonathan Butler, George Benson, and Anita Baker than classic jazz artists like Ella Fitzgerald or Joe Williams. Certainly these are artists that have been very influenced by jazz, but their delivery and accompanying band create a more modern take. The audience for more classic-sounding jazz of the big band era is fading.

CULTIVATING AN AUDIENCE AND GAINING EXPOSURE

In the day of the jazz greats, record companies took care of promotion for their artists. This could include newspaper articles, interviews, write-ups in music magazines such as Billboard, and advertisements on the radio or in local newspapers about an upcoming performance. Presently, promotion is basically in the hands of the artist, at least at first. If you record a CD, in order to promote yourself, you would need to pay a professional promoter to distribute your project to radio stations. As mentioned above, these radio stations are fewer and further between, and while they can present a great opportunity to be heard, many jazz stations are not open to playing unknown artists. In some cases, it may be as simple as the radio programmer saying, "We already have too many female vocalists CDs." I know this because I've heard it myself! The cost of a good promoter may be out of reach. Investigate other ways that you can be heard through the Internet. You can create a web page and music videos to help gain exposure. It helps if you have other experienced musician friends who are working frequently and who may be able to steer you in the right direction regarding a promoter or agent.

What About an Agent?

There was a time when agents were plentiful in the entertainment business. In smaller cities and towns, local agents may not have booked very famous performers but found a niche with local bands, local clubs, and local performance venues. In the 1960s and 1970s, jazz bands, along with pop and R&B groups, could work five to six nights a week. Musicians that were finished playing at midnight could walk across the street or drive to another nearby club to hear the band playing until 1 a.m. There were impromptu jam sessions during the last set where many musicians and singers might sit in. Keep in mind that radio was alive as well, and this is how audiences learned about new artists. They relied on popular DJs and radio personalities to curate new music for them and would then go to a brick-and-mortar record store to purchase the new music they learned about. People who drove to work, teenagers in their cars, and parents driving their kids around town all listened to the radio.

In the early 1960s, most American radio did not have set program categories regarding style—they generally played whatever was popular, regardless of genre. So you could hear singer Barbra Streisand singing a ballad, the Beatles next, Nat King Cole, Ella Fitzgerald, then the Supremes. Later this changed so that there were radio stations that featured one musical style, which is where we still are today. However, local radio station DJs were often open to playing the music of local performers and telling the audience where a band or singer was performing. This meant that at least on a local level, instrumentalists and vocalists could get some airplay and an announcement that would tell the listener when and where they were appearing.

Without this accessible and popular radio mechanism, artists need more help to get their music noticed and their names recognized. An agent promotes you and finds performance opportunities. For years, booking agents worked for the performer, representing the artist in regard to contracts and salary. A good agent cultivated careers. Smaller local agents would work with large agencies in larger cities. Together they could book a singer and bands into other cities around the country. As the economy changed, so did the music business. Some clubs shut down, while other clubs scaled down the performances to two or three nights. There was not as much live work, so available agents also dwindled. By the end of the 1980s, there were very few if any local agents to represent local acts. There was also a reversal in the role of the agent. Many agents no longer represented local artists but instead represented the club owners. There are of course still large recognized agencies that represent musicians, actors, models, and so forth, such as the William Morris Endeavor. But, in the majority of cases, jazz artists have to represent themselves, especially at the beginning of their careers. Only when you become better known to music listening audiences, with a track record of well-attended shows, will an agent consider representing you.

A good agent has to spend time to meet people, contacting newspapers, major music magazines, and notable clubs managers. They often, at the beginning, do the work of a publicist and a manager all at once. If you are appearing with your band or performing as a duo with a pianist, the agent has to firm up a contract for your salary. If you are booked in another city, the agent would ask for travel expenses including lodging. The agent generally takes a percentage of whatever you make on your gigs. But, until you have a reputable agent that is interested in promoting and working with you, you are basically on your own.

At least for the present, jazz artists that are serious and want to perform have to make phone calls to club managers. You should go out to as many local jazz performances as possible and network with local, active jazz musicians. Make sure you have a professional online presence with a website. Luckily, there are many services that can guide you through setting up your own website and you don't need to be a technological genius to figure it all out. Take a look at WordPress, Presskit, BandFrame, Squarespace, and so on. These services are low cost and can help you get your music out to the world with a professional look and feel. You can include videos on these sites, which are increasingly important for new artists. Be sure to write a good, meaningful bio. If you need help or assistance writing your bio, enlist a friend with writing skills to help you. It can be very difficult to write about yourself in a way that feels natural! Be sure to have both CDs and online streaming demos of your work. It is very important to have a professional-looking website as this will in many ways signal your legitimacy as a musician to external audiences.

PRESENT PERFORMANCE VENUES

Before you seek performance venues, do your research. You don't want to contact a venue booking agent about a show only to find out that the club only features punk rock! Find out more about the venue in regard to what kind of music is typically showcased. Check past shows and research the artists who have performed at the venue. Make sure that your sound and style will fit in with the venue. Before you approach clubs, have a clear idea of what your performance will look like. Will you be accompanying yourself on piano or guitar? Will you be a duo or a trio or more?

Don't approach clubs before you have already spent a lot of time rehearsing and putting together a strong set. Hopefully you will find friends who will rehearse and perform with you for free, but if not, know how much hired musicians will charge for rehearsals. Either way, when you are beginning as a jazz performer, you will need to rehearse before performing! It seems so obvious, but it's worth repeating. Economic situations for all practicing musicians are difficult unless you are a recognized star.

Nightclubs

Before you decide the clubs where you would like to perform, be sure to go there and watch a performance. Research how the act was booked into the club. Was it through a local agent? Find out who does the hiring for the room. Does the room have a decent sound system or will you need to bring your own? Of course you want yourself and the band to get paid for the evening performance, but how much will that be? Ask other working musicians what the going rate may be. Many years ago, the musicians' union was a strong force in regard to the pay of working musicians. There would be a pay scale that club owners would have to follow. Unfortunately the musicians' union and local branches have lost control of small venues and clubs and there is no such reliability. Often payment is based on attendance, which puts the onus on the performer. Don't expect venues to do more than the bare minimum to promote your show.

Have a price in mind that is fair for a three-hour or four-hour performance. Be prepared that the club owner may want to pay you less and
in some cases may tell you that, since you are unknown, in order to be
featured, you will have to pay rent for the room. Sometimes your pay is
only what comes in at the door and won't even cover rent of the room.
You will have to weigh your decisions on what is affordable for you and
the advantages of playing in a particular club. There is a certain amount
of paying your dues at the beginning. Playing to tiny audiences of friends
and family in small, unknown venues is all part of the game. Just treat
every performance as important, no matter who is or is not there. This
is part of being a professional musician.

Private Parties

The most lucrative gigs for musicians at the present time are private engagements. This would mean playing at wedding receptions
and private events. You will give up many weekends and evenings to
do these events, but "general business" gigs are one way to make a
living as a musician. The audiences are almost always appreciative,
and at least at a wedding, you will usually get a free meal! In order
to be a successful, in-demand wedding band, you must have a very
broad repertoire of past and present hits. Wedding bands and bands
for other events (bar and bat mitzvahs, birthday parties, corporate
events, etc.) must have a fun, energetic set list that covers many styles
of songs, from dance songs to slower ballads. A professional website is
imperative, as is a proven track record of showing up on time, being
easy to work with, and providing wonderful energy for guests. You
will need to have your own professional equipment and be able to set
it up. Build your reputation one gig at a time and you will eventually
find yourself being very in demand and possibly commanding highly
respectable prices!

Concerts and Recitals

In some cities, there are concert halls or smaller rooms that may be
open to having local talent. Check out local churches, fraternal organiza-

tions (Knights of Columbus, Elks Lodges), and even library event rooms to research opportunities to put together your own recitals.

House Concerts

House concerts provide the artist a great deal of flexibility. In many cities, homeowners have home concert series for newer artists. You can research these opportunities with a simple Google search, or ask other artists about their experiences. If your own home is big enough to start a concert series, or if you have a comfortable rehearsal space, consider setting up a concert series of your own. Be sure to book yourself into a space that is big enough for a performance and provides seating for an audience. Home concerts also may have much more limited equipment, so be sure to know well in advance if you need to provide your own PA. Do research on how you are paid for each performance. Some house concerts have a small guarantee (an amount you are certain to be paid regardless of attendance), and others pass the hat, relying totally on audience donations to pay the artists.

Coffee Houses

Some privately owned coffee and teahouses in local communities might not be able to afford to pay you much, but you would have the opportunity to perform for a wide range of audiences. Coffee houses are better suited to quieter, more laid-back sets.

PERFORMANCE GUIDELINES IN ALL VENUES

In all of these venues, you need to be mindful of your overall volume as well as the balance between you and your accompanist or the band. Club owners and other clients will have expectations regarding your performance, and you may not always know when they are unhappy with your act. They may not like your repertoire, sound, or even apparel. Not all of this is within your control. All you can do is have a relatively good understanding of what they expect and act accordingly. Sometimes owners will be cordial to you but you won't be asked back, and it's not always because you did anything wrong.

None of the above is intended to paint a negative picture of jazz today. However, you do need to be a realist when it comes to your life as a jazz musician. Jazz artists usually play jazz nightclubs and smaller rooms, at least at first. If you gain popularity and the places you perform are generally filled, then you may have other opportunities to tour and perform outside of America. Some of your venues may wind up being very large—even a concert hall! Jazz audiences outside of the United States are actually larger than here, particularly in Europe and Japan. If you pay your dues in the United States and build a following here, you may have amazing travel opportunities in your future!

Today's jazz singers that play an instrument have an advantage. If you are a strong player on guitar or piano, you can accompany yourself. Economically this is a plus in regard to working as a musician—you are only paying yourself. However, you must work equally hard at singing and playing your instrument if this is the path you wish to take. In order to avoid falling flat as a solo artist, you must take care to write careful arrangements of each of your songs. You are playing the part of every other instrument, and it can be hard to maintain momentum through a full set.

If you play any instrument well, you have the advantage of working in a band—perhaps sometimes just as an instrumentalist and at other times as both a vocalist and the instrumentalist. If you listen to newer jazz artists, you have probably heard of Diana Krall, pianist and singer, or Esperanza Spalding, bassist and singer. Harry Connick Jr. started out as a jazz pianist but also sang. Other vocalist/instrumentalists include Diane Schuur, Shirley Horn, and Nina Simone—all wonderful pianists who accompany or have accompanied themselves. One of the many newer artists is guitarist and vocalist Camila Meza, originally from Chile. Strongly influenced by her country's traditional songs, she combines jazz into her music. She is a talented guitar player as well as singer. You will often find that talented instrumentalists also sing (think of Louis Armstrong!). Modern instrumentalist/vocalist artists include Tony De-Sare, Daniela Schächter, John Pizzarelli, John Proulx, and Jamie Cullum to name a few. All of these artists are worth a careful listen.

CONCLUSION

As we review what you've learned in this book, remember that the history of blues and jazz, as well as the era in which it was very popular, helps us understand how jazz evolved and continues to evolve. Jazz vocal style entails specific stylistic considerations. Your delivery is more conversational; your phrasing more relaxed and laid-back. Instead of singing full voice through all of the phrases, you sing like you are having a personal conversation with someone. You want to tell a story through your performance and make an effort to connect to the audience through the lyrics of a song. Generally, you are not forcefully or theatrically singing. You will use gradual dynamics, and for the most part, held out notes are not belted. Jazz singing is a subtle and nuanced style, and as you become more experienced, you will find your own unique voice within the genre. In order to further your development as an artist, continue to listen to jazz with an educated knowledge of the idiom. The more we listen and the longer we listen, the more we begin to hear nuance in the music, and the more we know how to apply it to our own performances and practices.

As we learned in this chapter, there is no easy path to success as a jazz singer. This is not to say that there are not exceptions. Some talented artists are able to find a venue that works well right away and build from there. As in any art, jazz singing as a career can be difficult to sustain. It will take great determination on your part and a willingness to work extremely hard. Find ways to practice your art whether it is in your church, in the community, or in some of the aforementioned venues. Today's jazz vocalist's career may go down many winding roads. However, if you want to sing jazz, you will find a way.

INDEX

abdominis, transverse, 21–22
abduction, 24
ad lib. *See* rubato
african american brass bands, 10–11;
"Dr. Jazz," 11; " High Society," 11;
" Panama," 11
Aguilera, Christina, 93
alveoli, 18
American songbook characteristics:
structure, 119–20; medium tempo
swing, 120; up tempo swing, 120;
ballads, 120–21
aphonia, 25
Armstrong, Louis, 7, 9, 12, 65, 92,
98, 142–43
arrangements, 121–22
articulation, 8, 17, 32–34
arytenoids, 25
aural transcriptions, 141–42

back phrasing. *See* laying behind the
beat

Bailey, Mildred, 63–64
Baker, Chet, 15, 88, 92, 141, 143
ballad. *See* American songbook
characteristics
the bass, 90; "Willow Weep For
Me," 90; "Fascinating Rhythm,"
90; "There is No Greater Love,"
90; "In a Mellow Tone," 90; "I
Thought About You," 90; "Speak
Love," 90
bass listening. *See* the bass
bebop era, 15–16, 72–73
bebop vocal recording examples,
15; "One Note Samba" (Ella
Fitzgerald), 15; "Is You Is or Is
You Ain't My Baby" (Anita O
Day), 15l "Lullaby of Birdland"
(Mel Torme), 15; "Lullaby of
Birdland" (Sarah Vaughn), 15
beginning of swing, 11, 115–16
Bentyne, Cheryl, 122
big band era, 13

ABOUT THE AUTHOR

Jan Shapiro began her music studies at the Saint Louis Institute of Music and continued by earning her bachelor's degree, graduating cum laude from Howard University, Washington, D.C., and completing a master's degree from Cambridge College, Cambridge, Massachusetts.

Her first major engagement at the Playboy Club in Saint Louis lasted more than six months—until she and her group went on the road, touring extensively. Subsequently she performed at the Camellia Room in the Drake Hotel, Chicago; the Hyatt Hotels in Washington, D.C., and Atlanta; the Top of the Tower Club, New York City; Marriott Hotels in Florida, Washington, D.C., and St. Louis; the Chase-Park Plaza Hotel, St. Louis; various Sheraton Hotels and Ramada Inns; and numerous hotels, supper clubs, and jazz clubs in Boston and the New England area.

Jan was the guest vocalist for the prestigious Boston Globe Jazz Festival in 1987 and in 1990, leading off the festival in 1990.

As a musician, Jan has developed competence as a vocalist and flautist and on electric bass, piano, and keyboards as well as percussion. She is versatile in style, singing jazz, soft rock, pop, blues, and ballads with equal élan.

As a songwriter, she has written and collaborated in writing some of the songs she performs. In addition, she composed the score of *Tales of Toyland*, a children's production of Bob Kramer's Marionettes of Saint Louis, which toured nationally.

As a recording artist, she was the featured guest artist with the Airmen of Note—the official jazz ensemble of the U.S. Air Force—on a recording with international distribution. She has performed as a studio vocalist in recording numerous advertising jingles, TV spots, and demos, including recording with Len Dressler of the Singers Unlimited for the Broadway musical *Copperfield*. Jan has her own CDs: *Read Between the Lines*, *Not Commercial*, *Back to Basics*, and her new CD produced in 2012–2013, *Piano Bar After Hours*.

Jan was the recipient of the National Endowment of the Arts for jazz special projects in 1989–1990. She has published articles and research papers for the International Association of Jazz. In addition, Jan has contributed entries of early jazz artists to *Jewish Women in America: An Historical Encyclopedia*, *American National Biography*, and *Dictionary of American Biography*.

Jan was a former faculty member of the Voice Department at Fontbonne College, Saint Louis, Missouri, and in the Jazz Studies Department at Southern Illinois University, Edwardsville, Illinois. She is presently professor of voice at Berklee College of Music. She was also chair of the Voice Department at Berklee from 1997 through May 2010. She has presented vocal clinics around the country, including the International Association of Jazz Educators conferences, and adjudicated high school jazz choirs in the New England area.